FAMILY LAW PROTOCOL

The Law Society

The Law Society

© The Law Society 2002

ISBN 1 85328 885 3

Published by the Law Society
113 Chancery Lane
London WC2A 1PL

Typeset by J&L Composition Ltd, Filey, N. Yorks
Printed by TJ International Ltd, Padstow, Cornwall

Contents

The Law Society's
Family Law Protocol

Other titles available from Law Society Publishing:

Conveyancing Handbook (8th edition)
Frances Silverman
1 853 28695 8

Employment Law Handbook (July 2002)
Daniel Barnett and Henry Scrope
1 85328 716 4

Civil Litigation Handbook
Edited by John Peysner
1 85328 592 7

Elderly Client Handbook (2nd edition)
Gordon R. Ashton with Anne Edis
1 85328 467 X

Probate Practitioner's Handbook (3rd edition)
Edited by Lesley King
1 85328 517 X

Environmental Law Handbook (4th edition)
Trevor Hellawell
1 85328 721 0

All books from Law Society Publishing can be ordered through good bookshops or direct from our distributors, Marston Book Services, by telephone 01235 465656, fax 01235 465660 or e-mail *law.society@marston.co.uk*. Please confirm the price before ordering.

PART VI: Domestic abuse

66

Foreword

by Dame Elizabeth Butler-Sloss, President of the Family Division

Any litigation is stressful but all family practitioners recognise that family disputes are the most stressful of all disputes coming through the courts. The breakdown of marriage or other partnership and the issues that have to be resolved in the heat of the emotional turmoil of the failed relationship require the most careful and sensitive handling by judges, magistrates, practitioners and all who come into contact with the family.

The first port of call for litigants is the solicitor who often bears the burden of the high emotion frequently showing itself in corrosive anger and intense hostility towards the other party. It is of the utmost importance that solicitors in family cases have a clear understanding of the problems which arise in family disputes and how best to resolve them in the often over-charged atmosphere created by the litigants.

The Law Society is to be congratulated for producing this excellent Family Law Protocol which covers best practice in all aspects of private family law disputes. There is an important emphasis upon mediation, family dispute resolution and the interests of children in the family.

It provides an admirable and welcome guide to those who practise in this difficult and sensitive field and I am happy to endorse it.

Elizabeth Butler-Sloss
President

Preface

This book (the Protocol), published here for the first time, is made up of a series of protocols structured in a logical order and appended by other relevant guidance.

The main protocol, appearing as Part I, deals with matters that need to be considered in all family law cases.

Part II deals with matters to be considered in addition to those in Part I, when acting for clients in proceedings for divorce, judicial separation or nullity.

The approach to be taken in private law cases (involving individuals and children as opposed to cases where public authorities are involved) both where parents are married and where they are not, is covered in Part III. It is hoped that a protocol covering public law cases involving children will be published separately in due course.

Part IV covers protocols for ancillary relief, pre- and post-application. The Pre-Action Protocol, annexed to *Practice Direction: Court Bundles* (10 March 2000) is reproduced here and deals with matters prior to the issue of ancillary relief proceedings. The post-application protocol applies to steps in ancillary relief proceedings after an application to the court has been initiated (as implemented on 5 June 2000).

Financial issues in property and family law arising from cohabitation and its breakdown are covered in Part V.

Part VI applies to domestic abuse and includes advice on screening, making needs assessments and carrying out safety planning, as well as dealing with proceedings to ensure personal protection.

Mediation is covered in Part VII, including screening and the role of solicitors during mediation.

The Appendices include the President's Practice Direction on Court Bundles (Appendix 1), the SFLA Code of Conduct (Appendix 2), guidance given by the Advisory Board of the Children Act Sub-Committee of the Law Society on dealing with contact in cases where domestic violence has occurred (Appendix 3), the Protocol of the National Association of Child Contact Centres (Appendix 4) and useful contacts and addresses (Appendix 5).

AIMS OF THE PROTOCOL

1. To encourage a constructive and conciliatory approach to the resolution of family disputes.
2. To encourage the narrowing of the issues in dispute and the effective and timely resolution of disputes.
3. To endeavour to minimise any risks to the parties and/or the children and to alert the client to treat safety as a primary concern.
4. To have regard to the interests of the children and long-term family relationships.
5. To endeavour to ensure that costs are not unreasonably incurred.

SCOPE

This Protocol has been drafted by the Law Society's Family Law Committee with the active support and close involvement of the Solicitors Family Law Association (SFLA), the Lord Chancellor's Department (LCD) and the Legal Services Commission (LSC). Consultation was also undertaken to ensure that the views of practitioners and other interested parties were taken into account. The intention is that it should form a benchmark of good practice with which all solicitors practising family law in England and Wales should comply.

Many experienced family law solicitors will undoubtedly find that they already practise to the standard outlined in the Protocol, but even they may find it a helpful guide. For those solicitors who are newly qualified or less experienced, there will be much in this document that will assist them in their professional development in the practice of family law.

Lay members of the public representing themselves in situations of family breakdown may also find the document of help in showing the way in which matters should be approached and dealt with to minimise dispute and distress. It is also hoped that the judiciary will find it of assistance in indicating the expected standards to be practised by those appearing before them in family matters.

Compliance with this Protocol will become a requirement of membership of the Law Society Family Law Panel and the Solicitors Family Law Association Specialist Accreditation Panel.

This is the first edition of the Protocol. The intention is to update the document regularly to accommodate the changes in law and practice that will continue to take place. Users of this document are encouraged to write to the Law Society with comments on how they have found the Protocol to work in practice. Those views and comments will be of considerable help in reviewing this first edition.

It has to be recognised that the Protocol cannot override solicitors' duty to their clients or their duty as officers of the court. It is accepted that it will sometimes be impossible to comply with the Protocol because clients can refuse to take advice. Family matters are so diverse in content that any final decision on how to deal with a particular matter must remain at the discretion and judgement of solicitors themselves.

This Protocol must be read in conjunction with *The Guide to the Professional Conduct of Solicitors 1999*, published by the Law Society. All references to the *Guide* in this Protocol refer to the eighth edition.

Acknowledgements

The Law Society's *Family Law Protocol* was drafted by the following:

Kay Birch, *Lord Chancellor's Department*
Rosemary Carter, *Solicitors' Family Law Association*
Lynn Graham, *Legal Services Commission*
Mark Harper, *Chair of the Protocol Drafting Group*
David Hodson, *Solicitors' Family Law Association*
Kathryn Hughes, *Law Society*
Rose James, *Legal Services Commission*
Eileen Pembridge, *Law Society*
Peter Watson-Lee, *Law Society*
Sarah White, *Legal Services Commission*

The Protocol was endorsed by:

The Rt Hon The Lord Irvine of Lairg, *The Lord Chancellor*
The Rt Hon The Baroness Scotland of Asthal, *Parliamentary Secretary, Lord Chancellor's Department*
Rosie Winterton MP, *Parliamentary Secretary, Lord Chancellor's Department*
The Rt Hon Dame Elizabeth Butler-Sloss DBE, *President of the Family Division*
Steve Orchard CBE, Chief Executive, *Legal Services Commission*

Association of District Judges
Association of Lawyers for Children
Family Law Bar Association
Family Law Committee of the Law Society
Justices Clerks Society
Legal Services Commission
Lord Chancellor's Department
National Association of Child Contact Centres
Solicitors' Family Law Association
UK College of Family Mediators

PART I

Main protocol

I   THE FIRST MEETING

1.1   In all family law matters it is important that at the first meeting or early in the case, solicitors should consider certain matters.

Reconciliation

1.2   When instructed by clients facing family breakdown the first step (unless it is clearly inappropriate to do so), is to discuss with clients whether the relationship is over or whether there is a possibility of saving the relationship.

1.3   Solicitors must keep an up-to-date list of referral agencies including local marriage guidance agencies, counsellors, Relate, etc. and refer clients to them where appropriate. Solicitors need to bear in mind their clients' ethnic, cultural and/or religious background when considering referral agencies and should be aware of the benefits of referring clients to agencies with knowledge of their particular background.

1.4   The prospect of saving the relationship and/or the benefits of family or personal counselling or marriage guidance should be kept under review throughout the case.

Other support services

1.5   Solicitors should be aware of any support services (for example debt counsellors, contact centres, Citizens' Advice

Bureaux, organisations for persons with addictions and/or their families) which can assist clients in coming to terms with problems which underlie their relationship breakdown or have come about as a result of that breakdown. Solicitors should advise clients of the existence of these organisations and encourage clients to use their services when appropriate.

Family dispute resolution

1.6 If reconciliation appears to be unlikely, there are a number of ways to resolve disputes arising from family breakdown. When first instructed by clients, solicitors must:

(a) explore carefully clients' legal needs and establish exactly what clients are trying to achieve;

(b) establish whether clients' circumstances might affect the choice of a resolution procedure, for example cost or accessibility;

(c) consider the most appropriate form or forms of dispute resolution for the case or for individual parts of the case and keep them under review throughout the case.

1.7 The four most commonly used forms of dispute resolution in family cases are:

(a) agreement between the parties;

(b) negotiation between solicitors, including meetings between solicitors acting for each of the parties and their clients where appropriate;

(c) mediation or other forms of alternative dispute resolution (ADR);

(d) adjudication by the court.

These are often used in combination.

1.8 Solicitors must ensure that clients are aware that in financial matters an agreement must be embodied in a consent order to be directly binding on the other party.

Mediation

1.9   Solicitors must:

(a)   at an early stage, unless it is clearly inappropriate to do so, explain the mediation process and advise clients on the benefits and/or limitations of mediation in their particular case, as well as the role of the solicitor in supporting the mediation process;

(b)   keep the suitability of mediation under review throughout the case;

(c)   encourage clients to go to mediation when and where appropriate.

For more information and best practice relating to mediation see Part VII.

Domestic abuse

1.10   Solicitors must be aware of the widespread incidence of domestic abuse and the remedies available. Information and best practice guidance (including a definition of domestic abuse, the meaning of screening, needs assessment and safety planning) is provided in Part VI. Solicitors must:

(a)   treat the safety of clients and any children as a priority;

(b)   screen appropriately for domestic abuse;

(c)   where domestic abuse is not revealed at the first meeting, continue to keep the possibility of domestic abuse under review;

(d)   when domestic abuse is disclosed, undertake a needs assessment and safety planning with clients; the appropriate remedy for each client's individual needs must be discussed and kept under review.

Urgent issues

1.11   Solicitors need to establish the basic facts of a case, establish whether there are any urgent issues in addition to those mentioned above and advise on how it is appropriate to deal with them.

1.12   Examples of issues that may require consideration at an early stage are:

(a)   the need for interim maintenance to be agreed or applied for;

(b)   whether maintenance for children can be agreed or whether reference to the Child Support Agency (CSA) should be made;

(c)   the need for clients to be advised about welfare benefits;

(d)   the immediate housing needs of clients and any relevant children;

(e)   severance of a joint tenancy of a family home;

(f)   registration of rights of occupation of a family home (solicitors should advise clients that owners of property are now notified by the Land Registry if a matrimonial home notice or caution is placed on their property);

(g)   the need to make/revise wills, bearing in mind the intestacy rules, the effect of divorce on wills and the possibility of appointing testamentary guardians;

(h)   the need to close or freeze joint accounts or to make them joint signatory accounts;

(i)   the consideration of nominations for death in service benefits;

(j)   the need to consider an application under the Matrimonial Causes Act 1973, s.37 to prevent either the dissipation of assets or the giving of notice to quit by one of two joint tenants.

Children

1.13   In any case where the parties have dependent children, solicitors should exercise particular care and refer to Part III of this Protocol, even where there is no apparent dispute between the parents of the child or children. If there are child protection issues, whether arising from domestic abuse, child abduction or any other matters, the safety of the children should be treated as paramount.

1.14 In all children matters it is important for solicitors to bear in mind and to emphasise to clients, throughout the case, the continuing nature of the relationship of parent and child and the benefits that co-operation between the parents brings to the children.

1.15 When dealing with questions in respect of the upbringing of a child, solicitors always need to remember that the child's welfare is the court's paramount consideration (Children Act 1989, s.1(1)). Accordingly when acting for parents, solicitors must be prepared to advise their clients that the court will be approaching the matter from the viewpoint of what is best for the child and that this can override the wishes of either clients or children or both.

1.16 Solicitors should warn clients about the potentially damaging effects of involving their children in disputes concerning their parents and the particular risks of harm to the children where they are encouraged to take sides or become involved in their parents' disputes.

1.17 Solicitors should make clients aware that negotiations in relation to children are separate from negotiations in relation to other disputes they may have with the other parent on other issues. Correspondence relating to children issues in particular should be separate from correspondence relating to financial and other aspects or at least shown under separate headings. Clients should be made aware that the courts treat issues concerning children and issues concerning money, even if they relate to children, separately and independently.

1.18 Solicitors should use their best efforts to dissuade clients from making applications in respect of children when it is apparent that the applications are motivated by intentions other than consideration for the children's welfare. Examples are applications for contact or residence made from spite, from a wish to 'teach the other party a lesson' or from a perception that this would improve financial claims. Likewise, solicitors should attempt to dissuade parents from opposing an application for such reasons.

1.19   It is recognised that the Child Support (Maintenance Assessments and Special Cases) Regulations 1992, SI 1992/1815 (which provide for levels of child maintenance to be reduced by a specific proportion depending on the number of nights that the children are with the non-resident parent) may cause particular difficulty. Clients should be advised that the law relating to contact is separate and distinct from child support. Clients with residence should be discouraged from attempting to reduce contact and clients without residence should be discouraged from applying for increased contact when the prime purpose is to affect the child support to be paid.

1.20   Solicitors should encourage clients to consider what, when and how they intend to tell their children about a parental separation and encourage them to consider doing so with the other parent. In difficult cases couples may find that mediation or counselling on this single issue can be helpful although public funding for mediation is not available unless there is a dispute.

1.21   Solicitors should discuss with unmarried parents whether or not it is appropriate to enter into a parental responsibility agreement or seek a parental responsibility order, and/or make a will or appoint a testamentary guardian.

1.22   Solicitors should be aware of the benefits of parenting plans and should consider their use from the outset. Parenting plans were used successfully in the information meeting pilots run by the Lord Chancellor's Department. They are in the process of being revised and will be reissued at a future date.

1.23   During the course of a case relating to children, solicitors should be sensitive to suggestions from clients that a child is showing any signs of serious emotional disturbance. Solicitors should be able to refer where appropriate to other agencies that may be able to assist, for example the child's school, GP, health visitor or other healthcare professional, a counsellor, or any other agency that may be able to assist. Solicitors should be in possession of the names and addresses of these referral agencies.

Clients under a disability

1.24   Solicitors must bear in mind that they cannot be retained by clients incapable of giving instructions (*The Guide to the Professional Conduct of Solicitors 1999*, Principle 24.04). Incapacity includes those of a young age or those with learning disabilities, mental health problems, brain damage (including dementia) or any combination of these characteristics. A solicitor consulted by a client who cannot give instructions must identify a willing and suitable next friend or guardian ad litem to conduct any litigation (Family Proceedings Rules (FPR) 1991, SI 1991/1247, Rule 9.2). The Official Solicitor will act in the absence of anyone else willing and suitable (*Practice Note, Official Solicitor: Appointment in Family Proceedings* [2001] 2 FLR 155).

1.25   Equally, solicitors must be alert to any information suggesting that the other party may be under a disability and in need of a next friend or guardian ad litem. There are specific rules about service of a petition on a person under a disability (FPR 1991, Rule 9.3).

1.26   If a solicitor is in any doubt about whether a client (or the other party) is a patient for the purposes of FPR 1991, Rule 9.1 the Official Solicitor can provide a standard medical certificate to be completed by the person's medical attendant (see Appendix 5 for the address of the Official Solicitor).

The initial letter of retainer

1.27   At the commencement of every case solicitors should send to clients a letter of retainer confirming their instructions, the extent of their retainer and any limits placed upon them by clients. They should ensure that clients verify that the letters reflect accurately the instructions given, and understand the effects of the instructions and the limitations. The letter should normally be sent to the client following the first meeting.

1.28   If at any time during the conduct of cases a client decides to ignore advice given by a solicitor or to act in a way that the solicitor considers to be unwise or detrimental to that client's interests, the solicitor must write to the client expressing these concerns and the consequences of the action proposed by the client. In publicly funded cases solicitors should also consider costs (see paras. 2.1–2.15 below).

Provision of information

1.29 At the first meeting, or immediately thereafter, solicitors should consider what standard information clients might find helpful. In particular, solicitors should consider giving clients leaflets on matters relating to their particular dispute (see the Law Society's website at *www.lawsociety.org.uk* or Appendix 5 for contact details of Professional Ethics) or alternatively should at least make clients aware if such leaflets are available. Solicitors should also be aware that other organisations publish leaflets relevant to family matters. These include the Solicitors' Family Law Association, the Legal Services Commission, the Lord Chancellor's Department and the Court Service.

Advising on outcomes

1.30 At the end of the first meeting or at an early stage thereafter, solicitors should outline possible outcomes to clients in writing as far as this is practical on the information available. It is recognised that in cases where there has been little or no disclosure this outline will need to be very broad and this needs to be explained to clients. It is important that clients are not given unrealistic expectations: either of what can be achieved or of the time a matter may take to resolve.

2   COSTS INFORMATION

Introduction

2.1 Whether clients are privately or publicly funded, solicitors are reminded of their obligation to comply with the Solicitors' Costs Information and Client Care Code 1999 (Solicitors' Practice Rules 1990, Rule 15). A serious breach of the Code, or persistent breaches of a material nature, could be treated as professional misconduct and/or inadequate professional services. Breaches which create prejudice for the other party or for the court could result in costs penalties.

2.2   In particular, in accordance with the Code, solicitors must:

(a)   give clients the best information possible about the likely overall costs, including a breakdown between fees, VAT and disbursements (it is recognised that in family law matters such an estimate may need to be in broad terms at the commencement of a case);

(b)   discuss with clients how, when and by whom any costs are to be met and consider whether clients may be eligible for public funding;

(c)   discuss with clients, and keep in mind at all times, the principle of proportionality between the likely outcome and the probable expense of resolving the dispute, having regard also to the impact of any possible costs orders;

(d)   keep clients regularly updated about the level of costs.

Availability of public funding

2.3   Solicitors are reminded of their professional duty to consider and advise clients on the availability of public funding where clients might be entitled to such assistance. Accordingly, solicitors should be aware of the levels of eligibility for public funding. Although solicitors can discuss alternative methods of funding, if clients may be eligible this should be explained to them and they must be given the opportunity of applying for public funding. The availability of public funding must be kept under review throughout the matter.

2.4   In discussing the availability of public funding, solicitors must explain to clients the effects of the statutory charge, the possibility of contributions, the reporting and mediation requirements of public funding and the costs protection that being publicly funded may provide.

2.5   If clients who may be eligible for public funding either at the outset of a case or at any time during it have consulted solicitors who do not undertake publicly funded work, they must be given the option of being referred to solicitors who do carry out publicly funded work (even if this means referring clients to another firm). If clients eligible for public funding nevertheless wish to continue to instruct their original solicitors on a privately funded basis, the availability of public funding and their decision not to apply for it should be confirmed to clients in writing.

The requirements of public funding

2.6   When clients are publicly funded, solicitors need to be aware of the requirements of public funding, and in particular, make clients aware of the statutory charge, so as to ensure that clients are aware that there are circumstances in which solicitors' duties under publicly funded work can override their duty of client confidentiality. The solicitor is required to make a report to the Legal Services Commission, for example, where there is a belief that the publicly funded client requires the case to be conducted unreasonably or at an unjustifiable expense to the Community Legal Service Fund or where the solicitor is simply uncertain as to whether it would be reasonable to continue acting. A costs officer is entitled to disallow all subsequent costs following a failure to report and it is important that the client should be aware of this. On client confidentiality, solicitors are referred to Regulation 4 of the Legal Services Commission (Disclosure of Information) Regulations 2000/442 (see 1B-76 in the *Legal Services Commission Manual*, Volume 1) and Principle 5.03 of *The Guide to the Professional Conduct of Solicitors 1999.*

2.7   Solicitors are reminded of their duty to safeguard public funds and to ensure that the funding code criteria applicable to the case remains satisfied. Solicitors must ensure that they file and serve Notice of Issue of a Certificate of Public Funding and Notice of Discharge of that Certificate.

The statutory charge under public funding

2.8   Solicitors should consider and discuss with the client, where appropriate, the application of the statutory charge in cases which may result in the recovery or preservation of the possession of property (for example, the protection of a right of occupation of property or the unlocking of the value of property). Such cases can give rise to the statutory charge, even where the title to the property is not in issue (*Parkes* v. *Legal Aid Board* (1994) 2 FLR 850). Solicitors should remember that the charge does now apply where property is recovered or preserved for the benefit of a third party, such as a child, and may do so even where the case was funded under the Legal Aid Act 1988.

2.9   Solicitors should be aware that the statutory charge arises where property which was at issue is recovered or preserved. Where the parties have been able to agree throughout on the disposition of an item of property, the charge cannot attach to it. Solicitors should endeavour to narrow the subject matter of the dispute.

2.10   Solicitors should consider and discuss with the client, where appropriate, the possibility of postponement of the statutory charge where property which is to be used as the clients' home is recovered or preserved – including under the Trusts of Land and Appointment of Trustees Act 1996. It should be borne in mind that where the necessary conditions are met, including the payment of interest, the statutory charge over the property can be postponed until future sale and transferred onto the purchase of a new property from the proceeds indefinitely, ultimately reverting to the recipient's estate.

Costs orders

2.11   Solicitors must consider and explain to clients the factors which may affect the court in considering costs, including:

(a)   the conduct of litigation, for example, material non-disclosure of documents and delay in seeking disclosure or seeking excessive disclosure;

(b)   the absence of an offer or a counter-offer or an offer made too late to be effective;

(c)   the reasonableness of any offer or counter-offer – since unreasonable offers are not helpful and will not be viewed as such by the court.

11

2.12   Solicitors should consider and discuss with the client the costs implications of the provisions of the Family Proceedings Rules 1991 dealing with offers for settlement as set out at FPR 1991, Rule 2.69(a)–(h) inclusive. Solicitors should remember that the specific costs implications of Rule 2.69(b) and (c) apply only in respect of 'without prejudice' offers and consideration should always therefore be given as to whether an offer should be an open one or made without prejudice. Solicitors should remember, too, that the costs implications apply, not when beating one's own offer, but when beating the offer made by the other party. The potentially heavy costs and interest penalty which may flow if the final order is more advantageous to one party than either that party's offer or the offer of the other party, should also be noted.

2.13   In considering the implications of FPR 1991, Rule 2.69, clients should also be made aware that they could be penalised in costs for an unreasonable failure to:

(a)   make a timely and effective offer;

(b)   respond to an offer; and

(c)   make a counter-offer.

2.14   Solicitors are reminded of their obligation to provide costs estimates to the court in Form H as to the total costs incurred up to the date of the relevant hearing. In preparing such estimates, they should have regard to Section 6.5 of the CPR Costs Practice Direction, which provides that the amount of an estimate is a factor which may be taken into consideration on a detailed assessment of costs by a costs officer.

Instructing counsel

2.15   If solicitors propose to instruct counsel in respect of any aspect of the work on the case, the costs implications of doing so must be explained to the client and authority to instruct counsel secured from the client. The following points should also be kept in mind:

(1) In ancillary relief proceedings, an estimate of costs to date should be provided to counsel at all stages.

(2) In private paying cases, the solicitor should ensure that he or she has appropriate security for counsel's fees, remembering the personal obligation to be responsible for payment of the fees of counsel.

(3) The solicitor should remember that he or she has a duty to the client to negotiate with counsel's clerk to ensure that counsel's fees are fair and reasonable. The solicitor should seek the client's approval before concluding an agreement as to fees.

(4) In publicly funded cases, solicitors should be aware that the level of counsel's fees will impact upon any costs limitation and solicitors may need to provide verification to the Legal Services Commission of the work done by counsel to support a claim for fees under the Graduated Fee Scheme.

(5) Whenever counsel is to appear as an advocate on behalf of the client, the client must be aware, save in exceptional circumstances, of the identity of the barrister concerned and what arrangements are being made for attendance by any representative of the solicitor with counsel.

3 COMMUNICATION WITH THE OTHER PARTY AND WITH THE CLIENT

3.1 Solicitors, and parties where unrepresented, must show courtesy and solicitors must be professional in all communications with other solicitors or parties. Solicitors should not give personal opinions or comments within letters. Solicitors are referred to the SFLA's 'Guide to good practice on correspondence' obtainable from the Solicitors' Family Law Association (see Appendix 5 for contact details).

3.2 Communications must focus on identification of issues and their resolution. They should be clear and free of jargon. Protracted, unnecessary, hostile and inflammatory exchanges and 'trial by correspondence' must be avoided. The effect of correspondence upon clients and other family members should be considered so that correspondence sent by solicitors does not further inflame emotions or antagonise.

3.3 The impact of any correspondence upon its readers and in particular the parties, must always be considered. It is crucial that solicitors or parties do not raise irrelevant issues nor unreasonably cause other parties or their own clients to adopt an entrenched, polarised or hostile position.

3.4 Solicitors should consider, where possible, sending any substantive items of correspondence to clients for checking initially, particularly if that correspondence contains proposals for settlement. They should send copies of all but routine letters to their clients as a matter of course, unless there is specific reason not to do so.

3.5 Clients' circumstances are so varied that it would be difficult to prepare a specimen first letter to the other party. However, the tone of the initial letter is important. It should briefly address the issues and avoid protracted, clearly one-sided and unnecessary arguments or assertions. In drafting the first letter, solicitors must:

(a) where practicable, obtain approval from clients in advance;

(b) where writing to unrepresented parties, recommend that they seek independent legal advice, and enclose a second copy of the letter to be passed to any solicitor instructed.

3.6 Solicitors are warned that they should not use e-mail as a sole means of correspondence with other solicitors and of the danger of sending e-mail correspondence to a client whose spouse or partner might know and use their e-mail password. E-mail should not be used to correspond with clients unless the client has given an express assurance that it is a suitable means of correspondence. Solicitors are advised to consult the Law Society's 'Guidance for solicitors on the use of electronic mail' (April 2000) and 'Professional ethics and IT' (June 2000). These are both available from Professional Ethics on 0870 606 2577.

4 GIVING NOTICE OF ISSUE OF PROCEEDINGS

4.1 Prior to the issue of proceedings of any nature, solicitors acting for applicants or petitioners should notify those acting for respondents (or respondents where unrepresented) of the intention to commence proceedings at least seven days in advance, unless there is good reason not to do so. It is bad practice for proposed respondents then to issue proceedings to pre-empt proposed petitioners issuing, unless a good reason for doing so exists. If respondents nevertheless instruct their solicitors to issue, their solicitors must warn them of the court's disapproval of such action, the possible costs implications and the impact of such action on the rest of the case (see the SFLA's 'Guide to good practice on service', obtainable from the SFLA, and Appendix 5 for contact details).

5 WHERE PARTIES HAVE ALREADY REACHED AGREEMENT

5.1 Separating couples may have reached an agreement on a matter prior to seeing solicitors. The agreement may have been reached in direct negotiation between the parties, in mediation or by some other method. In such circumstances solicitors should do the following:

(1) Inform separating couples that they can only act for one party and that the other party should obtain independent legal advice.

(2) When first instructed send to clients a letter setting out, in full, the terms of their retainer and the limits placed upon it by the client. Particular care should be taken in confirming in writing any limits placed on the retainer by the client. Any modification of the retainer at a later stage should also be notified to the client in writing.

(3) Establish that the client fully understands the terms and effect of the agreement and the alternative options available.

(4)   Establish whether the agreement has been reached on the basis of full and frank disclosure and emphasise the dangers of incomplete disclosure (this is of particular importance in financial matters and a clear warning should be given to clients of the consequences of the making of financial orders).

(5)   Discuss with the client any omissions or points that need clarifying.

(6)   Advise the client on the implications of the agreement reached and whether it is in the client's best interests, both in the short term and the long term. This includes, where appropriate, advising on other options available. In doing this solicitors need to bear in mind all the implications including the benefits attached to settling on an amicable basis and the cost, risks and time involved in further negotiations, mediation or litigation (especially if the agreement is within the range that the court might order).

(7)   Solicitors should consider sending a disclaimer letter to the client for signature and return by the client in cases where the solicitor is concerned that there is inadequate disclosure or a clearly inadequate settlement. In the event that the client refuses to sign such a disclaimer letter, solicitors might consider whether this gives grounds for termination of retainer (see Principle 12.12 of *The Guide to the Professional Conduct of Solicitors 1999*.

5.2   If solicitors consider that duress or undue influence has been brought to bear on their clients to enter an agreement that is unreasonable or unfair, they should tell clients and advise them in writing to review the agreement. If the client refuses to do so then the solicitor should have regard to Principle 12.04 of *The Guide to the Professional Conduct of Solicitors 1999* which says: 'a solicitor must not accept instructions which he or she suspects have been given by a client under duress or undue influence'.

5.3   Solicitors should advise clients on the most appropriate way to record the agreement and, as appropriate, draft and present to the court any necessary consent order or prepare any necessary agreement/documents.

5.4 When drafting financial consent orders, solicitors should refer to the further guidance given in Part IV, paras. 16.1–16.6. Failure to advise fully and appropriately can result in negligence suits succeeding against the solicitors involved.

6   HUMAN RIGHTS

6.1 Solicitors must have knowledge of the Human Rights Act 1998, the Strasbourg jurisprudence and case law arising and must keep this knowledge up to date.

6.2 Solicitors should not use the Act inappropriately to bolster weak cases or to bring inappropriate points, but they must carefully consider, and keep under review, whether there is a general issue as to whether clients' human rights have been breached. If so, solicitors should discuss with clients what further action should be taken. Solicitors should consider the content of the *Practice Direction (Family Proceedings: Citation of Authorities)* [2000] 4 All ER 288.

7   GOOD PRACTICE GUIDANCE

7.1 Solicitors must comply with the Rules contained in *The Guide to the Professional Conduct of Solicitors 1999*, including the Law Society's Anti-Discrimination Rules and the SFLA Code of Practice (see Appendix 2).

7.2 The SFLA publishes guidance notes on good practice, which are updated regularly and there is currently guidance on:

    (a)   service

    (b)   correspondence

    (c)   disclosure

    (d)   acting for children

    (e)   working with the Bar

(f)   cases with an international element.

Copies are obtainable from the SFLA (see Appendix 5 for contact details). Solicitors should read and follow these guides.

PART II

Proceedings for dissolution of marriage – divorce, judicial separation or nullity

Solicitors should keep under review at all times the availability of public funding and the need to provide clients with costs information at the outset and on a regular basis.

1 SCOPE

1.1 This section covers all applications for divorce, judicial separation or nullity unless otherwise specified.

2 IN ALL MATTERS

2.1 Solicitors should always bear in mind the following:

(1) Family issues often go to the heart of people's religious, cultural or personal beliefs.

(2) Any procedure taken, for example the contents of a divorce petition or correspondence, may impact on other issues such as children and ancillary relief.

(3) The cultural and/or religious implications of divorce should be considered, for example the question of obtaining a 'get' or a 'talaq'. To some clients of particular faiths, obtaining a divorce according to their religion may be as important as a civil divorce. Certain faiths have stringent rules, set a timetable vis-à-vis a civil divorce or only allow a husband to apply. Solicitors must consider these issues and take such

steps as they reasonably can in the civil divorce to help clients to obtain a religious divorce.

(4) Issues that arose during the marriage which are irrelevant to the evidence of irretrievable breakdown but which may impact on children or ancillary relief issues should be dealt with by separate correspondence.

3 JUDICIAL SEPARATION OR NULLITY

3.1 Although applications for judicial separation or nullity are rare there will be circumstances where it will be impossible to obtain a divorce or where it is appropriate to obtain a decree of nullity or judicial separation. These may, in particular, be appropriate where clients have strong religious and/or cultural reasons for not wishing to divorce or in cases when a divorce decree would cause a loss of pension rights.

3.2 Where an application for judicial separation is appropriate, solicitors should discuss with clients the possible extra expense of obtaining a divorce after a decree of judicial separation. The ramifications of obtaining a judicial separation also need to be discussed, most particularly the ramifications in relation to pension benefits and the death of one of the parties to the marriage after judicial separation.

3.3 In cases where an application for nullity is appropriate, solicitors should discuss with clients the additional expense of obtaining a decree of nullity rather than one of divorce.

4 PRIOR TO ISSUING PROCEEDINGS

4.1 Prior to the commencement of proceedings solicitors should:

(a) check that the marriage of the parties is recognised in this country; and/or

(b) advise clients to confirm that a decree granted here will be recognised in the country in which they will live, so far as is practicable; and

(c)   in appropriate circumstances, consider which country or countries are the appropriate jurisdictions to issue proceedings for dissolution and if appropriate (see in particular European Council Regulation No. 1347/2000, commonly known as Brussels II), which is the most advantageous;

(d)   notify respondents' solicitors (or respondents where unrepresented) of the intention to commence proceedings at least seven days in advance, unless there are good reasons for not doing so (see para 4.1 of the main protocol in Part I above especially in regard to it being bad practice for respondents to use this notification to pre-empt the petitioners by issuing first);

(e)   provide respondents' solicitors (or respondents where unrepresented) with the fact or facts on which the petition is to be based and the particulars, with a view to coming to an agreement or minimising misunderstanding unless there is good reason not to do so.

4.2   Solicitors should ensure that a list of approved translators is kept in the office so that a speedy and accurate translation of a marriage certificate can be obtained if necessary.

5   THE PETITION

5.1   In drafting the petition the following guidelines should be followed:

(1)   Where the divorce proceedings are issued on the basis of adultery:

    (a)   petitioners should be encouraged not to name co-respondents and should be told that there is no need to do so in law;

    (b)   solicitors should advise respondents who do not intend to defend the proceedings that an admission of adultery on the acknowledgement of service is likely to be sufficient evidence (the need for separate confession statements should be avoided wherever possible).

(2)   Where the divorce proceedings are issued on the basis of unreasonable behaviour, petitioners should be encouraged only to include brief particulars sufficient to satisfy the court.

(3)   In all cases solicitors should consider carefully with clients the possible aggravating effect of claiming costs from respondents and such claims should only be made when it is considered appropriate.

5.2   The filing of answers and cross-petitions should be discouraged unless there are good reasons for doing so. Solicitors acting for respondents who are unhappy with the allegations made can record their client's concerns in correspondence so that the petitioner is aware of them. Where clients wish to defend allegations made in divorce petitions because they may be relevant on determination of ancillary relief or on children issues, the parties should be encouraged to enter into agreements that respondents will not defend the particulars raised in petitions and that petitioners will agree that respondents are free to raise their concerns afresh in the ancillary relief or children proceedings. This agreement should be made within correspondence.

5.3   Respondents to petitions must be discouraged from filing another petition in the same or another court unless for very good reason, for example inordinate delay in proceeding with the petition.

6   THE STATEMENT OF ARRANGEMENTS FOR CHILDREN

6.1   The Statement of Arrangements form is an important document and must be completed carefully. The court cannot fulfil its statutory obligations unless this form is completed fully.

6.2   Before filing the Statement of Arrangements for children:

(a)   a copy should normally be sent to respondents' solicitors (or respondents where unrepresented) for approval and a reasonable time should be allowed for reply;

(b)   the other party's signature should be obtained where possible;

(c)   only information necessary to state the arrangements being made for the children should be included;

(d)   solicitors should discuss with clients the arrangements being proposed for the children to ensure that the interests of the children are not overlooked. Clients should be encouraged to discuss and agree arrangements for parenting with their spouses where appropriate.

7   APPLYING FOR DECREE ABSOLUTE

7.1   Before applying for decree absolute solicitors should consider whether circumstances exist which make it advisable to delay finalising a decree of divorce until these issues are resolved (for example outstanding issues relating to pension entitlement or life insurance). Solicitors acting for respondents should consider asking petitioners' solicitors to agree in advance that petitioners will not apply for a decree absolute if this course of action would prejudice respondents.

7.2   Solicitors acting for respondents on divorce must discourage their clients from making inappropriate applications for decree absolute and make it clear that an inappropriate application may be penalised in costs.

7.3   Clients should be advised that they may be prejudiced, both in terms of law and procedure, if they remarry after decree absolute but before an application for ancillary relief is made on their behalf.

PART III

Children (private law)

Solicitors should keep under review at all times the availability of public funding and the need to provide clients with costs information at the outset and on a regular basis.

1 SCOPE

1.1 This section applies to all private law cases involving children, with the exception of cases relating to adoption, whether these cases are brought under the Children Act or otherwise. Some of the matters contained within this Protocol are to be found within the Family Proceedings Rules 1991, SI 1991/1247 and the Family Proceedings Courts (Children Act 1989) Rules 1991, SI 1991/1395 ('the Rules') and their inclusion within the Protocol is for reinforcement in view of their importance.

2 PROTECTIVE MEASURES AND CONFIDENTIALITY

2.1 In cases concerning allegations of child abuse, whether physical, sexual or emotional, solicitors should, wherever possible, encourage clients to inform the appropriate authority. Solicitors should consider this paragraph in conjunction with para 2.4 below.

2.2 Solicitors should be aware of local support agencies (for example counselling agencies) and be able to signpost clients to any agencies which may be of assistance to them or their children.

2.3   The courts now give greater consideration to the impact on children of domestic violence against a parent (see *Re L, V, M and H* [2000] 2 FLR, 334; the ruling in *Re D (Contact: Reasons for Refusal)* [1997] 2 FLR 48 also refers to the fact that there can be good reasons for implacable hostility). Clients should not be pressed into agreeing contact in circumstances where they genuinely believe it is not in the interests of the children to see the absent parent or where the absent parent is using the proceedings to continue their harassment. The effect on children of seeing someone being subjected to domestic violence or of being alone with the perpetrator of violence should be borne in mind (see the Report to the Lord Chancellor by the Advisory Board on Family Law: Children Act Sub-Committee on the question of parental contact in cases where there is domestic violence, published 12 April 2000 and reproduced at Appendix 3). Advice should be realistic but sufficiently robust to support clients should their individual circumstances raise questions about the appropriateness of contact.

2.4   Solicitors should be aware of and, in appropriate circumstances, must make clients aware of, the effect of Principle 16.02 (note 4) of *The Guide to the Professional Conduct of Solicitors 1999*, which states the exceptional circumstances in which solicitors should consider revealing confidential information to an appropriate authority:

> 'There may be exceptional circumstances involving children where a solicitor should consider revealing confidential information to an appropriate authority. This may be where the child is the client and the child reveals information which indicates continuing sexual or other physical abuse but refuses to allow disclosure of such information. Similarly, there may be situations where an adult discloses abuse either by himself or herself or by another adult against a child but refuses to allow any disclosure. The solicitor must consider whether the threat to the child's life or health, both mental and physical is sufficiently serious to justify a breach of the duty of confidentiality.'

Solicitors are reminded that they are obliged to disclose the whereabouts of a child who is the subject of a seek and find order, regardless of the rules of client confidentiality.

2.5   However, solicitors should always bear in mind that they owe a duty of confidentiality to their clients and may have to justify any breach of that duty to their professional body. It is always advisable to seek advice from the Law Society's Professional Ethics section (tel. 0870 606 2577 and see Appendix 5 for contact details), other members of the profession, partners in the firm and professional insurers.

3   ABDUCTION

3.1   Solicitors must be aware of the emergency steps that need to be taken if a child is abducted, in particular the procedure to make an application without notice and the court's powers under s.33 of the Family Law Act 1986 in relation to disclosure of the whereabouts of a child. Solicitors should appreciate that an order under this section may be directed to persons who are not parties to any proceedings within which the order is made. Solicitors should in addition be aware of s.34 of the Family Law Act 1986 which gives a court the power to order recovery of a child (including physically taking charge of them using such force as is necessary and delivering the child to the appropriate person).

3.2   Solicitors should be aware of the difference between abduction cases within the United Kingdom and international abduction cases.

3.3   Solicitors must recognise that international child abduction is a specialist area of law and that they should take specialist advice. Solicitors should consider discussing all cases of child abduction (except within England and Wales) with the Lord Chancellor's Department's Child Abduction Unit (see Appendix 5 for contact details). Proceedings should be heard by a full-time High Court judge wherever possible. Solicitors should remember that the law and procedures in Scotland and Northern Ireland are different and will be relevant in cross-border cases.

3.4   In the event that a child is abducted (or is suspected to have been abducted) from this country to another which is party to the Hague Convention, solicitors should forthwith contact the Lord Chancellor's Department's Child Abduction Unit (see also *Re: H: Abduction: Habitual Residence: Consent* (2000) 2 FLR 294, which gives a useful exposition of the Child Abduction and Custody Act 1985, the Hague Convention of 1980 and the issue of habitual residence and consent). The LCD will fax across appropriate forms which solicitors should complete with clients and return whereupon the LCD will forward them to the appropriate country with a view to an application for return being made.

3.5 Solicitors must be aware that if a child is abducted from abroad into England and Wales, non-means, non-merits tested public funding is available to an applicant whose application under the Hague Convention or the European Convention has been submitted to the Child Abduction Unit, pursuant to s.3(2) or s.14(2) of the Child Abduction and Custody Act 1985 (Funding Code Criterion 11.13). Other applications for public funding will be subject to means and merits criteria under the Funding Code.

3.6 Solicitors must advise unmarried fathers that unless they have obtained parental responsibility or there is an application before the court for parental responsibility and a prohibited steps order, abduction of the child from the United Kingdom will not be a wrongful removal under the Hague Convention.

4   CHILD CONTACT CENTRES

4.1 Child contact centres are a valuable (although limited) resource and solicitors should be aware of their local centres and the facilities and services which they provide. Child contact centres have agreed to adhere to a set of National Standards. The Protocol for Referrals has been developed by the National Association of Child Contact Centres and endorsed by leading members of the judiciary (see Appendix 4).

4.2 The majority of child contact centres provide supported contact whereby contact can take place in the centre or children can be handed from one parent to the other. Consideration should also be given to the appropriateness of arranging a handover using third parties and keeping parents apart with no face-to-face contact with each other.

Solicitors should explain to clients the difference between supported and supervised contact before the first contact visit at a centre occurs.

4.3 Where violence is an issue, careful thought should be given to the use of child contact centres. In cases of domestic violence (especially where there have been criminal proceedings or injunctive relief) supervised contact will generally be necessary, at least initially. There are a small number of child contact centres which undertake high vigilance supervision and the National Association of Child Contact Centres (NACCC) have details of their member centres which provide this service (see Appendix 5 for contact details). It is often useful for clients to visit the child contact centre before the first contact period takes place.

4.4 Contact centres are not equipped to deal with abusers who pose a serious threat to their families and it is vital that the centre co-ordinator is given the full background (orally, if necessary) in order to decide whether the centre can accommodate the family. Referral forms must be completed as fully and accurately as possible. It is important that contact centres have full information about details of violent or abusive behaviour.

4.5 Solicitors must make it clear on referral forms if other family members can be present during the contact visit. Solicitors for the resident parent should discuss with them the need to prepare the child for the visit.

4.6 Solicitors have a duty of confidentiality to their clients and cannot reveal details about their client without the client's consent. If clients refuse to give consent to reveal information required on the referral form, a referral should not be made.

4.7 No contact centre can guarantee that a child will not be removed from it. It is vital that centres are warned if there is a fear of this or if there have been threats of abduction. If so, solicitors should discuss with the resident parent giving the centre recent photographs of the children and of the contact parent, if possible. If there is a possibility of abduction abroad, solicitors for parents with residence should be asked to retain the passports of parents having contact and/or those of the children to ensure safe contact can take place.

4.8   If it is not possible to access an appropriate contact service then the issue of face-to-face contact should be carefully reviewed. Other forms of contact might be suggested such as letters, telephone calls and the use of audio or video tapes. In serious cases, consideration should be given to whether it is appropriate to seek an order for no contact.

4.9   Solicitors should advise their clients that they should inform centres when they no longer need to use them. Clients should be made aware that child contact centres are regarded by the court as a temporary solution to difficulties in contact and not a permanent arrangement.

4.10   Solicitors should make clients aware that, in general, volunteers and staff at child contact centres do not provide reports or statements for any type of court proceedings unless a child is believed to be at risk of harm. However, a few supervised child contact centres are an exception to this general rule.

5   MEDIATION

5.1   Solicitors should recognise that alternative methods of dispute resolution such as mediation can be particularly helpful in dealing with disputes over contact and residence, especially where there are no welfare issues and the matter in dispute is the length or frequency of contact.

5.2   It is recognised that the availability of mediation and alternative dispute resolution varies across the country. Mediators offering both publicly funded and privately funded family mediation are available across England and Wales. This network of mediators is able to offer mediation for disputes over issues regarding children (including contact and residence).

5.3   Where out of court (independent) mediation is readily available, solicitors should consider referring clients to such mediation before issuing an application at the court. Where only court-based mediation or conciliation schemes managed by CAFCASS are available once proceedings have been issued, it may be necessary to issue proceedings early on.

6 BEFORE ISSUE OF PROCEEDINGS

6.1 Court proceedings should normally only be commenced if all reasonable avenues have been considered and found to be inappropriate or unworkable.

6.2 Solicitors should be aware of the CAFCASS *Practice Note (March 2001)* [2001] 2 FLR 151 and particularly the need to consider whether a child needs to be legally represented in the proceedings.

6.3 Solicitors should advise their clients on the most appropriate forum in which to commence proceedings (High Court, County Court, Family Proceedings Court) bearing in mind restrictions for publicly funded clients.

6.4 The LCD has recently published a set of leaflets for children and parents affected by relationship breakdown to help children of different ages to understand and cope with the changes that are occurring and to assist parents in discussing matters with them. The leaflets are available from FREEPOST, PO Box 2001, Burgess Hill, West Sussex, RH15 8BR or from *parentsandchildren@accelerated-mail.co.uk*.

7 ISSUE OF PROCEEDINGS AND THEREAFTER

7.1 Form C1 or other documents should be simply worded using non-inflammatory language and setting out clearly the order sought.

7.2 No evidence should be filed until ordered by the court as stated in the Family Proceedings Courts (Children Act 1989) Rules 1991, SI 1991/1395.

7.3 Solicitors must be aware that while many cases turn on events which occurred in the past, the statements in a children case should be as non-inflammatory as possible. They should advise clients that judges will be more concerned about plans for the future of a child than about past events. However they must be aware of the judgments in the cases of *Re L, V, M & H (Contact: Domestic Violence)* [2000] 2

FLR 334, which set out the limited circumstances where the history of a familial relationship will be relevant in contact proceedings. Solicitors are referred generally to the *Practice Direction on Case Management (31 January 1995)*, to be found at [1995] 1 FLR 456.

7.4   Clients must be advised that a court will have regard, inter alia, to the ascertainable wishes and feelings of the child concerned, considered in light of that child's age and understanding.

7.5   Solicitors must advise their clients about the need for confidentiality in proceedings relating to children and the fact that documents produced for proceedings relating to children, particularly the report of the Children and Family Reporter (CAFCASS Officer), may not be disclosed to those who are not parties to the proceedings without permission of the court (Family Proceedings Rules 1991, SI 1999/1247, Rule 4.23 and Family Proceedings Courts (Children Act 1989) Rules 1991, SI 1991/1395, Rule 23).

7.6   Solicitors should advise clients on the need (if any) for witnesses, and should discourage clients from a proliferation of witnesses who add nothing to the case. Solicitors are referred generally to the *Practice Direction on Case Management (31 January 1995)* [1995] 1 FLR 456, para 3.7.3).

7.7   Solicitors should advise clients that it will not assist them to produce statements written by their children nor to bring their children to speak with solicitors acting for one or other parent. Solicitors should not see the children who are the subject of any case in which they are advising unless they are acting for the child.

7.8   Solicitors should avoid drafting statements using emotive and/or inflammatory language and/or expressing subjective opinions. They should ensure that statements drafted reflect as closely as possible the client's instructions, particularly when there are language difficulties. Where English is not the first language, solicitors should always consider whether an interpreter should be present throughout an interview. Solicitors should consider whether they can act for a client when they do not speak the language of the client and no interpreter is available.

8 WELFARE REPORTS

8.1   Clients should be advised of the role of the Children and Family Reporter (CAFCASS officer) or local authority social worker in the decision-making process and the importance of the officer's report. Clients should be encouraged to co-operate with the reporter and advised that failure to do so could prejudice their case.

8.2   Solicitors should be aware of and, where appropriate, advise clients on the right of a child to apply to be joined as a party to the proceedings in the event that the Children and Family Reporter (CAFCASS Officer) is unable or declines to represent the wishes of the child in a way that the child deems appropriate.

9 EXPERTS

9.1   Permission from the court must be sought before an expert is appointed (see *Re: A (Family Proceedings: Expert Witnesses)* [2001] 1 FLR 723).

9.2   Recent and relevant experience on the part of the expert is essential. A curriculum vitae should be sought from the proposed expert.

9.3   Experts should only be instructed and indeed their evidence will only be admitted where necessary, that is in cases where other available evidence does not deal with the relevant issue and where the welfare of the child dictates that such further evidence ought to be obtained.

9.4   Solicitors should advise clients that they should not take children to appointed experts, nor obtain experts' reports without prior permission from the court.

9.5   Parties should be encouraged to use a single expert jointly instructed if this is appropriate in the circumstances of the case. The costs of such an expert should be apportioned between the parties. When clients are publicly funded, solicitors must report to the Legal Services Commission if clients will not agree to the use of a single expert where that would be appropriate to the case. The joint instruction of experts should be encouraged in appropriate cases. The letter of instruction will fall to one of the parties to prepare and its contents should be agreed (if possible) by the other parties. The letter of instruction, whether agreed or not is disclosable.

9.6 Where the identity of an expert is agreed the parties should agree a joint letter of instruction. Judicial guidance in respect of the instruction of experts is to be found in *Re: CS (Expert Witnesses)* [1996] 2 FLR 115 and more recently in the case of *Re: CB and JB (Minors) (Care Proceedings: Guidelines)* [1998] 2 FLR 211. See also *Practice Note (Re: R (A Minor) (Experts' Evidence)(27 July 1990))* [1991] 1 FLR 291; the Children Act Advisory Committee Annual Report 1994/95 and in particular, the guidance given in respect of the joint instruction of experts in Children Act cases; and finally, the Children Act Advisory Committee 'Handbook of Best Practice in Children Act Cases' (Lord Chancellor's Department, 1997).

9.7 Solicitors need to be aware of the provisions of Principle 16.02 (note 5) of *The Guide to the Professional Conduct of Solicitors 1999* and their duty to disclose experts' reports in proceedings under the Children Act 1989. The full text of note 5 is reproduced below.

'5. In proceedings under the Children Act 1989 solicitors are under a duty to reveal experts' reports commissioned for the purposes of proceedings, as these reports are not privileged. The position in relation to voluntary disclosure of other documents or solicitor/client communications is uncertain. Clearly advocates are under a duty not to mislead the court (see 21.01 at p.374). Therefore, if an advocate has certain knowledge which he or she realises is adverse to the client's case, the solicitor may be extremely limited in what can be stated in the client's favour. In this situation, the solicitor should seek the client's agreement for full voluntary disclosure for three reasons:

(i) the matters the client wants to hide will probably emerge anyway;

(ii) the solicitor will be able to do a better job for the client if all the relevant information is presented to the court;

> (iii) if the information is not voluntarily disclosed the solicitor may be severely criticised by the court.
>
> If the client refuses to give the solicitor authority to disclose the relevant information, the solicitor is entitled to refuse to continue to act for the client if to do so will place the solicitor in breach of his or her obligations to the court.'

Clients should be advised of the above.

9.8 Whether or not an expert is instructed jointly, that expert must be prepared to answer reasonable questions raised by any party.

10   MANAGEMENT OF COURT PROCEEDINGS

10.1 It is recognised that there are a variety of court practices throughout the jurisdiction in managing Children Act cases and that any guidelines on the management of cases will be affected by this. The following can therefore only be a broad overview.

10.2 If not automatically provided, solicitors should consider seeking a directions hearing and/or a dispute resolution/case management hearing in order to identify and minimise the areas of dispute.

10.3 Both parties' solicitors should inform the court listing section as soon as it becomes clear that a case's time estimate has changed and provide a revised time estimate.

10.4 Solicitors must produce court bundles in accordance with the *Practice Direction (Family Proceedings: Court Bundles)* [2000] 1 FLR 536 reproduced at Appendix 1.

10.5 Solicitors should attempt to agree in advance with other parties any evidence which is undisputed and inform the court of agreed facts in accordance with the *Practice Direction* cited above.

10.6 Solicitors must, where necessary, obtain an appropriate direction of the court to ensure the attendance of the children and family reporter, as provided in the Family Proceedings Rules 1991.

10.7   Solicitors must be aware and make their clients aware that they will need to exercise restraint when questioning a reporting officer, although cross-examination of children and family reporters is now provided for in the Family Proceedings Rules 1991.

11   AFTER THE CONCLUSION OF PROCEEDINGS

11.1   Solicitors must write to clients confirming the outcome of proceedings and return, where available, any original documents which clients have provided.

11.2   Solicitors must remind clients of the confidential nature of the proceedings and any relevant documents.

11.3   Solicitors should advise clients of the mechanism for review of decisions and, unless clearly inappropriate, remind them of the possibility of mediation as a means of resolving further disputes.

11.4   Where solicitors have given an undertaking in relation, for example, to safekeeping of documents, they should remember to seek to have the undertaking discharged at the conclusion of proceedings.

11.5   Solicitors should consider with their clients how the child is to be told the results of proceedings, particularly when the child has expressed views which have not been accepted by the court.

PART IV

Protocols for ancillary relief

PRE-APPLICATION PROTOCOL FOR ANCILLARY RELIEF

1 INTRODUCTION

1.1 The Pre-Application Protocol was annexed to *Practice Direction (Ancillary Relief Procedure)* [2000] 1 FLR 997, and implemented with the new rules for ancillary relief on 5 June 2000. It was produced in consultation with the Law Society and is reproduced in full below as part of this *Family Law Protocol*.

1.2 It applies to all applications for ancillary relief and financial provision as defined in FPR 1991, Part 1, Rule 1.2(1) and/or other applications for ancillary relief.

1.3 Note that the numbering is not consistent with the rest of this Protocol and for clarity's sake will appear in a different font.

1. Introduction

1.1

1.1.1 Lord Woolf in his final Access to Justice Report of July 1996 recommended the development of pre-action protocols:

'to build on and increase the benefits of early but well informed settlement which genuinely satisfy both parties to a dispute'.

1.1.2   Subsequently, in April 2000, the Lord Chancellor's Ancillary Relief Advisory Group agreed this pre-application protocol.

1.2   The aim of the pre-action protocol is to ensure that:

(a)   Pre-application disclosure and negotiation takes place in appropriate cases.

(b)   Where there is pre-application disclosure and negotiation, it is dealt with

i.   cost effectively;
ii.   in line with the overriding objective of the Family Proceedings (Amendments) Rules 1999;

(c)   The parties are in a position to settle the case fairly and early without litigation.

The court will be able to treat the standard set in the pre-application protocol as the normal reasonable approach to pre-application conduct. If proceedings are subsequently issued, the court will be entitled to decide whether there has been non-compliance with the protocol and, if so, whether non-compliance merits consequences.

2.   Scope of the Protocol

2.1   This protocol is intended to apply to all claims for ancillary relief as defined by FPR 1991, Rule 1(2). It is designed to cover all classes of case, ranging from a simple application for periodical payments to an application for a substantial lump sum and property adjustment order. The protocol is designed to facilitate the operation of what was called the pilot scheme and is from 5 June 2000 the standard procedure for ancillary relief applications.

2.2   In considering the option of pre-application disclosure and negotiation, solicitors should bear in mind the advantage of having a court timetable and court managed process. There is sometimes an advantage in preparing disclosure before proceedings are commenced. However solicitors should bear in mind the objective of controlling costs and in particular the costs of discovery and that the option of pre-application disclosure and negotiation has risks of excessive and uncontrolled expenditure and delay. This option should only be encouraged where both parties agree to follow this route and disclosure is not likely to be an issue or has been adequately dealt with in mediation or otherwise.

2.3   Solicitors should consider at an early stage and keep under review whether it would be appropriate to suggest mediation to the clients as an alternative to solicitor negotiation or court-based litigation.

2.4   Making an application to the court should not be regarded as a hostile step or a last resort, rather as a way of starting the court timetable, controlling disclosure and endeavouring to avoid the costly final hearing and the preparation for it.

First Letter

2.5   The circumstances of parties to an application for ancillary relief are so various that it would be difficult to prepare a specimen letter of claim. The request for information will be different in every case. However, the tone of the initial letter is important and the guidelines in paragraph 3.7 should be followed. It should be approved in advance by the client. Solicitors writing to an unrepresented party should always recommend that he seeks independent legal advice and enclose a second copy of the letter to be passed to any solicitor instructed. A reasonable time limit for a response may be 14 days.

Negotiation and Settlement

2.6   In the event of pre-application disclosure and negotiation, as envisaged in paragraph 2.2 an application should not be issued when a settlement is a reasonable prospect.

Disclosure

2.7   The protocol underlines the obligation of parties to make full and frank disclosure of all material facts, documents and other information relevant to the issues. Solicitors owe their clients a duty to tell them in clear terms of this duty and of the possible consequences of breach of the duty. This duty of disclosure is an ongoing obligation and includes the duty to disclose any material changes after initial disclosure has been given. Solicitors are referred to the Good Practice Guide for Disclosure produced by the Solicitors Family Law Association (obtainable from the Administrative Director, 366A Crofton Road, Orpington, Kent BR2 8NN).

3. The Protocol

General Principles

3.1   All parties must always bear in mind the overriding objective set out at FPR 1991, Rule 2.51B and try to ensure that all claims should be resolved and a just resolution achieved as speedily as possible without costs being unreasonably incurred. The needs of any children should be addressed and safeguarded. The procedures which it is appropriate to follow should be conducted with minimum distress to the parties and in a manner designed to promote as good a continuing relationship between the parties and any children affected as is possible in the circumstances.

3.2   The principle of proportionality must be borne in mind at all times. It is unacceptable for the costs of any case to be disproportionate to the financial value of the subject matter of the dispute.

3.3   Parties should be informed that where a court exercises a discretion as to whether costs are payable by one party to another, this discretion extends to pre-application offers to settle and conduct of disclosure. (Rule 44.3 Paragraph 1 of the Civil Procedure Rules 1998.)

Identifying the Issues

3.4   Parties must seek to clarify their claims and identify the issues between them as soon as possible. So that this can be achieved they must provide full, frank and clear

39

disclosure of facts, information and documents which are material and sufficiently accurate to enable proper negotiations to take place to settle their differences. Openness in all dealings is essential.

Disclosure

3.5   If parties carry out voluntary disclosure before the issue of proceedings the parties should exchange schedules of assets, income, liabilities and other material facts, using Form E as a guide to the format of the disclosure. Documents should only be disclosed to the extent that they are required by Form E. Excessive or disproportionate costs should not be incurred.

Correspondence

3.6   Any first letter and subsequent correspondence must focus on the clarification of claims and identification of issues and their resolution. Protracted and unnecessary correspondence and 'trial by correspondence' must be avoided.

3.7   The impact of any correspondence upon the reader and in particular the parties must always be considered. Any correspondence which raises irrelevant issues or which might cause the other party to adopt an entrenched, polarised or hostile position is to be discouraged.

Experts

3.8   Expert valuation evidence is only necessary where the parties cannot agree or do not know the value of some significant asset. The cost of a valuation should be proportionate to the sums in dispute. Wherever possible, valuations of properties, shares etc. should be obtained from a single valuer instructed by both parties. To that end, a party wishing to instruct an expert (the first party) should first give the other party a list of the names of one or more experts in the relevant speciality whom he considers are suitable to instruct. Within 14 days the other party may indicate an objection to one or more of the named experts and, if so, should supply the names of one or more experts whom he considers suitable.

3.9 Where the identity of the expert is agreed, the parties should agree the terms of a joint letter of instructions.

3.10 Where no agreement is reached as to the identity of the expert, each party should think carefully before instructing his own expert because of the costs implications. Disagreements about disclosure such as the use and identity of an expert may be better managed by the court within the context of an application for ancillary relief.

3.11 Whether a joint report is commissioned or the parties have chosen to instruct separate experts, it is important that the expert is prepared to answer reasonable questions raised by either party.

3.12 When experts' reports are commissioned pre-application, it should be made clear to the expert that they may in due course be reporting to the court and that they should therefore consider themselves bound by the guidance as to expert witnesses in Part 39 of the Civil Procedure Rules 1998.

3.13 Where the parties propose to instruct a joint expert, there is a duty on both parties to disclose whether they have already consulted that expert about the assets in issue.

3.14 If the parties agree to instruct separate experts the parties should be encouraged to agree in advance that the reports will be disclosed.

Summary

3.15 The aim of all pre-application proceedings steps must be to assist the parties to resolve their differences speedily and fairly or at least narrow the issues and, should that not be possible, to assist the Court to do so.

POST-APPLICATION PROTOCOL FOR ANCILLARY RELIEF

Solicitors should keep under review at all times the availability of public funding and the need to provide clients with costs information at the outset and on a regular basis.

2 AIM

2.1 The aim of this section is to ensure that disclosure, negotiation and ancillary relief proceedings take place cost effectively and in line with the overriding objective as defined in FPR 1991, Rule 2.5 (1B).

3 MAINTENANCE PENDING SUIT

3.1 At an early stage in proceedings solicitors should consider with the client whether or not an application for maintenance pending suit is appropriate (taking account of the costs and unpredictability of such applications).

3.2 Solicitors should consider whether the parties can reach an interim agreement either of their own accord, by negotiation between solicitors or by mediation. In the event that agreement does not seem a reasonable prospect an application for maintenance pending suit and/or interim periodical payments should be issued.

3.3 The issue of maintenance pending suit and/or interim periodical payments can be dealt with by consideration of the parties' budgets and on submissions only. Although no specific form is required for the sworn statement accompanying the application, solicitors may wish to consider appending to that statement Form E or part thereof showing the parties' respective incomes and expenditure.

3.4 Solicitors are reminded that legal fees payable by a client may be viewed in some cases as recurring expenses of an income nature which can be included as part of an application for interim periodical payments. If these are being applied for, solicitors should secure from their clients an undertaking to account to their solicitors for that part of the periodical payments order that reflects the legal fees.

4 FORM A

4.1 The notice of application should include all financial orders that the applicant might seek. Solicitors must remember that a pension sharing order must be applied for specifically. As soon as possible, solicitors for the party filing Form A should provide information to the other party as to which particular orders sought in Form A will be pursued.

4.2 Where an application is made in respect of property that is subject to a mortgage, a copy must be served on the mortgagees.

4.3 An application for pension sharing or attachment must be made in Form A as required by the Family Proceedings Rules 1991, Rule 2.70. Where details of the pension are available initially, the application should be specific about the order being sought against each individual pension policy. Where insufficient details are available, the application should be made in general terms. Form A should be amended once details are available. It should be borne in mind that this will involve additional fees.

4.4 A copy of Form A must also be served on any pension provider where a pension sharing or an attachment order is sought. When serving Form A solicitors should ask the pension provider to clarify whether they would deal with a pension sharing order internally or request an open transfer to another pension provider.

5 PENSIONS

5.1 Solicitors should be aware of the need to obtain details from pension providers and of the duties imposed upon pension providers to give these responses.

5.2 Where an application for pension attachment or sharing is likely to be relevant, solicitors should, where possible:

    (a)   obtain basic disclosure information, including the scheme rules, scheme booklet, early retirement and commutation terms);

    (b)   obtain the CETV (Cash Equivalent Transfer Value);

    (c)   send a blank page 10 of Form E for the pension provider to complete;

    (d)   consider taking advice from an appropriately qualified specialist, subject to the complexity of the issues and the costs involved;

    (e)   obtain confirmation from the pension provider that the arrangement proposed by the parties can be implemented;

    (f)   obtain an estimate of the costs involved in implementation of any order or agreement.

6   DISCLOSURE

6.1   Subject to the provisions of FPR 1991, Rules 2.61B(6) and 2.61D(3), the parties have an obligation to make full and frank disclosure of all material facts, documents and other material information relevant to the issues. Solicitors should tell their clients in clear terms of this obligation and of the possible consequences of breach of this obligation. This duty of disclosure is an ongoing obligation and includes the duty to disclose any material changes after initial disclosure has been given.

6.2   If clients wish not to disclose a fact or issue which is relevant to the proceedings, solicitors are bound by their duty of confidentiality to clients. Solicitors also have a duty not to mislead the court. If non-disclosure of a fact or issue is likely to involve solicitors in misleading the court, solicitors must terminate their retainer. The effect of this must be fully discussed with clients as early as possible.

6.3   Solicitors should follow the SFLA's 'Guide to good practice on disclosure' (see Appendix 5 for contact details).

7   EXPERTS

7.1   The guidance on experts contained in the Pre-Application Protocol for Ancillary Relief (see Part IV at para. 1.3 above, protocol sections 3.8–3.14) must be followed.

7.2   Part 35 of the Civil Procedure Rules 1998, SI 1998/3132 on expert evidence applies to ancillary relief proceedings.

7.3   Wherever possible, the parties should agree a joint letter of instruction.

7.4   While it may be necessary to obtain a broad assessment of the value of an asset, for example a shareholding in a private company, a precise valuation of an asset which will not be sold will not always be necessary.

7.5   Solicitors must ensure that all professional witnesses are instructed to avoid a partisan approach and to maintain proper professional standards.

8   FORM E

8.1   Solicitors (or parties where unrepresented) must include full details of their clients' financial assets, income and future needs when completing Form E, in order to enable identification of the issues and resolution of those issues prior to the Financial Dispute Resolution (FDR) hearing to allow it to have a good chance of success. The completed form should be as comprehensive and clear as possible and should give details of the contribution by each party to the marriage in the form of provider and/or homemaker.

8.2   If clients complete Form E, solicitors are still obliged to check the forms to ensure, as far as is praticable, that the information provided is full, complete and accurate. It is not good practice to exchange Forms E with sections incomplete. In the event that the value of an asset cannot be ascertained by the date that a Form E is due to be exchanged, information should be given to the other party's solicitors as to when the request for the information was made and when it is likely to be received.

8.3 Details of conduct by the other party should only be included in paragraph 4.4 of Form E when that conduct is sufficiently exceptional to be relevant.

9 STATEMENT OF ISSUES

9.1 The Statement of Issues must set out the issues in dispute between the parties on which the court is being asked to make adjudication. Where major issues have been agreed, this should be indicated briefly in the statement. Statements of Issues should be reviewed before the FDR hearing and again before the final hearing.

9.2 Where unnecessary or irrelevant issues are raised in the Statement of Issues, and pursued, costs can be awarded against the offending party and solicitors should make this clear to any clients who wish to raise such irrelevant issues.

9.3 Solicitors must also bear in mind the overriding objective in relation to ancillary relief proceedings: the requirement that cases are to be dealt with in a way which is proportionate to the amount involved. A matter may be relevant but disproportionate in costs terms to pursue. For example, it may not be proportionate to seek a detailed valuation of a family business that is not to be sold, although the existence of the business would be relevant to the way in which the dispute is resolved. However, some kind of valuation of the business may perhaps be necessary following the judgment in *White* v. *White* [2000] 2 FLR 981.

9.4 Solicitors are reminded of their duty to safeguard public funds and to report clients to the Legal Services Commission in the event that they fail to take account of the need to act in accordance with that duty.

10 FIRST APPOINTMENT

10.1 Solicitors must:

(a) ensure that clients are aware of the need to attend the first appointment once the date is fixed;

(b) ensure that clients are aware that the appointment can last for some hours, especially where the appointment is used as a Financial Dispute Resolution (FDR) hearing;

(c) discuss with clients, well in advance of completing Form G, whether it will be possible and appropriate to use the first appointment as an FDR;

(d) file and serve Form G, Statements of Issues, chronologies and questionnaires 14 days before the first appointment;

(e) discuss with clients in advance of the first appointment the likely directions to be requested from the district judge;

(f) in the event that the first appointment is treated as an FDR, comply with Part IV, para. 11.1 of the Protocol (see below) as far as possible.

10.2 Solicitors must provide a copy of the costs estimate in Form H to the court at the hearing and to clients at or before the first appointment and explain to them the significance of that form.

10.3 If it is intended to seek an order for costs at the hearing, the solicitor must also prepare the CPR Statement of Costs (Form N260) and file and serve this at least 24 hours before the hearing so that the costs can be assessed. If the client against whom costs would otherwise be sought is publicly funded, the other party may nevertheless seek an order for costs under the Community Legal Service (Costs) Regulations 2000, SI 2000/441, reg. 9(2) or (3). The court will need to have enough information before it to decide that it would have made a costs order if the client had not been publicly funded. If so, the court may decide there and then what the client should pay as long as it has enough information before it to determine:

(a) what is reasonable for the client to pay; and

(b) either what the full costs are or, that whatever they are, they are more than the amount the client has been ordered to pay.

Otherwise it has to decide in principle that the client should pay the costs and postpone the determination of the amount.

10.4 Solicitors attending the first appointment must have full knowledge of the case.

10.5 Solicitors should give consideration to seeking permission, in appropriate cases, for the filing of affidavits giving a broader presentation of the historical background to the case as evidence. These affidavits could include:

(a)   the respective contributions of the parties;

(b)   the source of current resources;

(c)   the standard of living during the marriage;

(d)   the main issues in dispute; and

(e)   the financial conduct of the parties.

This is to enable the court to consider all the circumstances of the case as required by the Matrimonial Causes Act 1973, s.25.

10.6 Solicitors must be aware that additional enquiries may be disallowed by the court where they do not relate to the Statement of Issues. The necessity to make further enquiries must be balanced by a consideration of what the enquiries will realistically achieve and the increased costs which are likely to be incurred by making them. Solicitors must also be aware that additional enquiries after the first directions appointment cannot be made save with permission of the court.

11   FINANCIAL DISPUTE RESOLUTION HEARING

11.1 Solicitors must:

(a)   ensure that clients are aware of the need to attend the Financial Dispute Resolution (FDR) hearing;

(b)   ensure that clients are aware that the appointment can last all day and that they will be available;

(c)   encourage clients to make offers and proposals in advance of the FDR appointment;

(d)   where they are recipients of offers and proposals, encourage clients to give them proper consideration and respond to them when possible to do so;

(e)   discuss with clients before the FDR what their 'bottom line' is likely to be, bearing in mind the delays and costs likely to be involved in the absence of settlement;

(f)   explain to clients the requirement to use their best endeavours to reach agreement and the judge's power to impose costs sanctions where one party refuses to make proposals or counter-proposals;

(g)   not seek or encourage parties to seek to exclude from consideration at the appointment, either separately or together, any such offer or proposal;

(h)   not pressure clients to accept offers they are not satisfied with at the FDR;

(i)   confirm subsequently, in writing, any current offer where there is no settlement at an FDR;

(j)   if acting for applicants, file with the court details of all offers and proposals and responses made to and by applicants not less than seven days before the FDR;

(k)   supply a costs estimate in Form H to the court at the hearing and also ensure that it is provided to clients and explained to them.

11.2   If the clients are seeking a costs order the CPR Statement of Costs (Form N260) also needs to be filed and served at least 24 hours before the hearing so that costs can be assessed. If the client against whom costs would otherwise be sought is publicly funded, the other party may nevertheless seek an order for costs under the Community Legal Service (Costs) Regulations 2000, SI 2000/441, reg. 9(2) or (3). The court will need to have enough information before it to decide that it would have made a costs order if the client had not been publicly funded. If so, the court may decide there and then what the client should pay as long as it has enough information before it to determine:

(a)   what is reasonable for the client to pay; and

(b)   either what the full costs are or that whatever they are, they are more than the amount the client has been ordered to pay.

Otherwise it has to decide in principle that the client should pay the costs and postpone the determination of the amount.

11.3   If not applied for at the first appointment, solicitors should give consideration to seeking permission to file an affidavit as outlined at para. 10.5 above.

11.4   Parties or their solicitors must not disclose the contents of FDR appointments or negotiations on the day, nor refer to them afterwards on an open basis in the proceedings. Evidence of anything said or of any admission made during the FDR appointment will not be admissible in evidence, except at the trial of a person for an offence committed at the appointment or in the very exceptional circumstances indicated in *Re D (Minors) (Conciliation: Disclosure of Information)* [1993] 1 FLR 932.

11.5   Advocates attending the FDR must have full knowledge of the case and should bear in mind the possibility that an FDR can be a lengthy hearing that can overrun. They should also bear in mind the need to negotiate and should consider carefully whether they can attend more than one FDR in the space of one day.

11.6   After an FDR solicitors should ensure that the district judge has removed from the file any correspondence relating to offers of settlement.

12   PREPARATION FOR THE FINAL HEARING

12.1   Solicitors must comply with *Practice Direction (Family Proceedings: Court Bundles)* [2000] 1 FLR 536 (see Appendix 1, below). Solicitors must be aware that this Practice Direction applies not only to final hearings but also to all other hearings specified within the Direction. It can be helpful at the earliest opportunity to prepare and keep updated a bundle for exchange. This can then form the basis of a trial bundle where necessary.

12.2 Not less than 14 days before the date fixed for the final hearing, solicitors for the applicant must file an open statement setting out the concise details and amounts involved of the orders which they propose to ask the court to make. Seven days after that the respondent must file a similar open statement. The offer and counter-offer must be served on the other party and filed at the court in accordance with the FPR 1991, Rule 2.69(e).

12.3 Applicants' solicitors, in conjunction with counsel, if counsel will be the advocate at the hearing, must prepare in advance of the final hearing and, where possible, agree with the solicitors acting for respondents:

(a) a concise statement of the remaining issues between the parties;

(b) a chronology of material facts.

12.4 In cases estimated to last for five days or more, and in which no pre-trial review has been ordered, an application should be made for a pre-trial review where practicable, at least three weeks before the hearing. Where possible, this should be conducted by the judge or district judge before whom the case is likely to be heard and should be attended by the advocates who are to represent the parties at the hearing. Where possible, all statements of evidence and all reports should be filed before the review and in time for them to have been considered by the parties (see *Practice Direction: Case Management* [1995] 1 FLR 456).

12.5 As with the first appointment and the FDR, solicitors must supply a costs estimate in Form H to the court at the hearing and ensure that it is provided to clients and that it is explained to them. If the case is likely to last for one day or less and the clients are seeking a costs order, the CPR Statement of Costs (Form N260) also needs to be filed and served at least 24 hours before the hearing so that costs can be assessed, unless the other party is publicly funded.

13   EVIDENCE

13.1   Evidence must be confined to relevant facts and matters which are material to the application. Where affidavit evidence is filed the deponents must be available for cross-examination on notice from the other party.

13.2   If any further evidence is necessary it must be confined to such matters as answering any serious allegation made by the other party, dealing with any serious issue raised or setting out any material change of circumstances. Evidence should be confined to issues which have been identified and in accordance with the directions given.

14   COSTS AND THE STATUTORY CHARGE

Costs

14.1   Solicitors must keep in mind at all times the principle of proportionality between the amount at stake and the amount which it is appropriate to spend on resolving the dispute.

14.2   Solicitors must consider and explain to clients the factors which may affect the court in considering whether to order costs, either in their favour or against them. These include:

(a)   conduct of the litigation, for example, material non-disclosure of documents and delay in seeking disclosure or seeking excessive disclosure;

(b)   the absence of an offer or a counter-offer or an offer made too late to be effective;

(c)   the reasonableness of any offer or counter-offer since unreasonable offers are not helpful and will not be viewed as such by the court.

14.3   In particular, solicitors should consider and discuss with clients the implications of the Family Proceedings Rules 1999, SI 1999/1247 dealing with offers of settlement, and the costs implications of this course of action (see FPR 1991, Rule 2.69 and following).

14.4 Solicitors should further consider and discuss with clients the implications of the principles set out in FPR 1991, Rule 2.69(a)–(e) inclusive, but most particularly in Rule 2.69(c) under which clients can be penalised in costs for unreasonable failure to:

(a) make a timely and effective offer;

(b) respond to an offer; or

(c) make a counter-offer.

14.5 Solicitors should remember that the specific costs implications of Rules 2.69(b) and (c) apply only in respect of 'without prejudice' offers and consideration should always, therefore, be given as to whether an offer should be an open one or made without prejudice. Solicitors should remember too that the costs implications apply, not when beating one's own offer, but when beating the offer made by the other party. Regard should also be had to the potentially heavy costs and interest penalty which may flow if the final order is more advantageous to one party than either that party's offer or that of the other party.

14.6 Solicitors are reminded of their duty to safeguard public funds and to ensure that the Funding Code Criteria applicable to the case remains satisfied. Solicitors must ensure that they file and serve Notice of Issue of a Certificate of Public Funding and Notice of Discharge of that Certificate.

14.7 In cases where clients are in receipt of public funding solicitors need to be aware of the requirements of public funding. In particular, they need to ensure clients are aware of the statutory charge and that they understand that there are circumstances in which solicitors' duties under publicly funded work can override their duty of client confidentiality. The solicitor is required to make a report to the Legal Services Commission, for example, where there is a belief that the publicly funded client requires the case to be conducted unreasonably or at an unjustifiable expense to the Community Legal Service Fund or where the solicitor is simply uncertain whether it would be reasonable to continue acting. A costs officer is entitled to disallow all subsequent costs following a failure to report and it is important that the client should be aware of this. On client confidentiality, solicitors are referred to the Legal Services Commission (Disclosure of Information) Regulations 2000, SI 2000/442, reg. 4 and to Principle. 5.03 of *The Guide to the Professional Conduct of Solicitors 1999.*

The statutory charge

14.8 Solicitors should consider and discuss with the client, where appropriate, the application of the statutory charge in cases which may result in the recovery or preservation of the possession of property (for example, the protection of a right of occupation of property or the unlocking of the value of property). Such cases can give rise to the statutory charge, even where the title to the property is not in issue (*Parkes* v. *Legal Aid Board* [1994] 2 FLR 850). Solicitors should remember that the charge does now apply where property is recovered or preserved for the benefit of a third party, such as a child, and may do so even where the case was funded under the Legal Aid Act 1988.

14.9 Solicitors should be aware that the statutory charge arises where property which was at issue is recovered or preserved. Where the parties have been able to agree throughout on the disposition of an item of property, the charge cannot attach to it. Solicitors should endeavour to narrow the subject matter of the dispute.

14.10 Solicitors should consider and discuss with the client, where appropriate, the possibility of postponement of the statutory charge where property which is to be used as the clients' home is recovered or preserved – including under the Trusts of Land and Appointment of Trustees Act 1996. It should be borne in mind that where the necessary conditions are met, including the payment of interest, the statutory charge over the property can be postponed until future sale and transferred onto the purchase of a new property from the proceeds indefinitely, ultimately reverting to the recipient's estate.

15 APPLICATIONS FOR VARIATIONS OF MAINTENANCE ORDERS

15.1 The procedure for variation applications is as set out in the Ancillary Relief Rules, without any special modifications.

15.2 On a variation application, it may be important, in order to save costs, to use the first appointment as an FDR in appropriate cases.

15.3 Solicitors must warn clients that fully contested variation applications are rarely proportionate in terms of the costs incurred. Clients should be encouraged to negotiate and settle without the need for a final hearing.

16 CONSENT ORDERS

This section must be read in conjunction with paras. 5.1–5.4 of the main protocol (see Part I).

16.1 Solicitors should take particular care in drafting financial consent orders, including recitals, ensuring that the consent order comprehensively reflects all terms agreed and resolves all financial issues between the parties. The Solicitors Family Law Association Precedents for Consent Orders (see Appendix 5 for contact details) are universally used and accepted and have been approved by members of the judiciary. Solicitors should use those precedents whenever appropriate to avoid unnecessary mistakes in drafting being made.

16.2 Solicitors must be aware of the limits of the court's power with regard to undertakings and should explain to clients the nature and power of an undertaking. Undertakings in consent orders are an essential part of placing each person under an obligation where there is not a statutory remedy available to deal with the point agreed, such as payment of life policy premiums or seeking release of a person from their obligations under a mortgage. This practice was explained and given impetus by Lord Brandon in *Livesey* v. *Jenkins* [1985] FLR 813, HL. The Law Society and the SFLA support this approach. Although doubts have been expressed as to the enforceability of non-financial under-takings it is best practice to use them and to ensure that clients sign personally all consent orders and statements of information.

16.3   When a consent order is filed, solicitors should ensure that each party has filed a Form A. The application filed by the party whose claims are being dismissed should be marked 'for dismissal purposes only' (this is accepted practice in the Principal Registry but it is not necessarily accepted practice throughout England and Wales). In the event that an application is made for dismissal purposes, solicitors making that application should consider what should be included in it.

16.4   In certain courts, when undertakings are given by a client, solicitors should be aware that consent orders are to be endorsed by solicitors to the effect that they have explained the effect of an undertaking and the consequences of its breach to their client.

16.5   Where a pension sharing or attachment order is to be made, the draft consent order should be sent to the pension provider for approval, to check that the terms and wording agreed can be implemented.

16.6   Solicitors should be aware of the very strict time limits and essential requirements concerning pension sharing and attachment orders in FPR 1991, Rule 2.70.

PART V

Cohabitation

Solicitors should keep under review at all times the availability of public funding and the need to provide clients with costs information at the outset and on a regular basis.

1   SCOPE

1.1   English law does not recognise cohabitation as a defined legal status. As yet, very few rights exist for cohabitants. However, in practice increasing numbers of the population live together without marrying. The problems they face on relationship breakdown are often similar to those faced by couples who have married. The lack of a single statute to deal with cohabitants can make the task of resolving those problems complex.

1.2   Much of the Protocol applies equally to cohabiting couples as it does to married couples. In particular, the approach contained in the main protocol (see Part I) and in the sections relating to children, domestic abuse and mediation are equally relevant to cohabitation breakdown.

1.3   However, in the area of finances, the options available to cohabitants differ greatly. This section of the protocol deals mainly with financial claims which arise on cohabitation breakdown, including same sex relationships.

2 ADVICE AT THE COMMENCEMENT OF OR DURING COHABITATION

2.1 Experience shows that many clients are unaware of their legal position when they cohabit and they often have misconceptions as to the rights or lack of rights that they may have. Clients may consult solicitors either at the commencement of their relationship or during it and solicitors should use such opportunities to explain to clients their legal position.

2.2 Sometimes clients may seek advice at the commencement of a relationship. If so, clients should be encouraged to consider entering into a cohabitation agreement, parts of which may be enforceable through the courts, if such an agreement would be beneficial to the clients. Solicitors should have access to precedents for cohabitation agreements at all times (model cohabitation agreements can be found in *Cohabitation Law and Precedents*, Sweet and Maxwell, 1999). Solicitors must advise clients that they can only act for one of the parties in drawing up such an agreement and that the other party must be separately represented.

2.3 Often clients will consult solicitors when they are intending to purchase a property together. In such circumstances, careful consideration needs to be given as to how the property should be owned. Solicitors must discuss with clients the implications of owning a property either as joint tenants or tenants in common and whether a deed of trust is desirable and/or whether they want to enter into a cohabitation agreement.

2.4 Where cohabitants decide to prepare a deed of trust at the time of purchase of a property, solicitors can only act for both cohabitants in preparing the deed if it is clear that there is an agreement from the outset as to all the terms of the deed and there is no conflict of interest.

2.5 At all relevant times, solicitors should advise clients who cohabit about the importance of making wills, making pension and death in service benefit nominations, considering life assurance policies and the benefits of parental responsibility agreements. Solicitors should also advise as to what might occur in the event that these matters are not dealt with.

3 ADVICE FOLLOWING RELATIONSHIP BREAKDOWN

3.1 At the first meeting or early on in the case, solicitors should consider and advise, where appropriate, on all the matters referred to in the main protocol (see Part I). The sections relating to reconciliation and other support services apply equally to cohabitation.

3.2 The paragraphs relating to family dispute resolution and mediation are also equally applicable in cohabitation cases. Accordingly, solicitors must, at an early stage, unless it is clearly inappropriate to do so, explain the mediation process and advise clients on the benefits and/or limitations of mediation in their particular case as well as the role of solicitors in supporting the mediation process. The suitability of mediation should be kept under review throughout the case and clients should be referred to mediation when and where appropriate.

3.3 The rest of the main protocol will also apply equally to cohabitation cases and should be referred to. It is important that solicitors screen appropriately for domestic abuse and consider whether there are any urgent issues to be dealt with. The list of examples of such urgent issues in the main protocol (see Part I, paras. 1.11 and 1.12) applies equally to cohabitation (with the exception of interim maintenance which is not available to unmarried parties).

3.4 Paragraphs 1.13–1.23 of the main protocol as to children (see Part I) and paragraph 1.29 as to the provision of information are equally applicable to cohabitation cases, although it is acknowledged that the availability of standard information for cohabitants is not as wide as for other family matters.

3.5 Under para. 1.30 of the main protocol it is important that solicitors should, at the end of the first meeting or at an early stage, outline the possible remedies that are available and the possible outcomes, as far as this is practical with the information available. It is important that clients are not given unrealistic expectations of what can be achieved nor unrealistic expectations of the time the matter may take to resolve.

3.6 Solicitors should advise clients that they might have claims in both property law and family law. Property law may deal with claims for a beneficial interest in a property by way of constructive or resulting trusts dealt with under the Trusts of Land and Appointment of Trustees Act 1996 ('Trusts of Land Act'), or proprietary estoppel and equitable accounting. If the couple have children, the clients may have claims under Children Act 1989, Schedule 1 and the Child Support Act 1991. Practice and procedure for property law and family law claims are very different, the former being governed by the Civil Procedure Rules 1998, SI 1998/3132, the latter by the Family Proceedings Rules 1991 and the Family Proceedings Courts (Children Act 1989) Rules 1991, SI 1991/1395.

3.7 Requirements for solicitors to provide costs information as outlined in the main protocol (see Part I, paras. 2.1–2.15) apply equally to cohabitation cases.

3.8 The provisions within the main protocol as to communications with the other party, the giving of notice of issue of proceedings, the steps to be taken when parties have already reached agreement and awareness of human rights law are all applicable to cohabitation cases.

4 PRIOR TO ISSUING PROCEEDINGS

Voluntary disclosure and mediation

4.1 Solicitors must consider and discuss the following with clients:

(1) The option of pre-application disclosure and negotiation. An application must not be issued when settlement is a reasonable prospect. Solicitors are referred to the Pre-Application Protocol for Ancillary Relief (sections 2.1–2.4, reproduced in Part IV of this

Protocol. Making an application to the court should not be regarded as a hostile step or a last resort but rather as a way of starting the court timetable, controlling disclosure and endeavouring to avoid the cost of final hearing.

(2)   The most appropriate form of dispute resolution for the case, based on clients' needs and individual circumstances, at an early stage. Solicitors must discuss mediation with clients, except where it is inappropriate to do so, and advise on whether it is likely to be suitable to their case and, where appropriate, refer them to an appropriate mediator (see Part VII on Mediation).

Identifying the issues

4.2   Solicitors must seek to clarify the parties' claims and identify the issues between them as soon as possible. To achieve this they must provide, as soon as possible, a full, frank and clear disclosure of facts, information and documents which are material and sufficiently accurate to enable proper negotiations to take place to settle their differences. Openness in all dealings is essential.

5   PRE-ACTION PROTOCOL

Civil Procedure Rules 1998, SI 1998/3132

5.1   Although there is no protocol specific to Trusts of Land Act 1996 cases, solicitors (or parties where unrepresented) must comply with the Protocols Practice Direction which applies to all types of civil cases and therefore to cohabitants in proceedings under the Trusts of Land Act 1996 (which are not covered by any approved protocol).

5.2   The common objectives of all the pre-action protocols are as follows:

(a)   to encourage the exchange of early and full information between the parties about any dispute between them which might need resolution by a court;

(b) to enable the parties to avoid proceedings by agreeing a settlement of the claim before the commencement of proceedings either through negotiation directly between them, with or without the assistance of a mediator if appropriate, or negotiation between the solicitors;

(c) to support the efficient management of proceedings where litigation cannot be avoided.

5.3 Accordingly, the court will expect the parties and their legal advisers to act reasonably in exchanging information and documents relevant to the claim and generally to try to avoid the necessity for the commencement of proceedings (in accordance with the overriding objective and the matters referred to in CPR 1998, Rule 1.1(2)(a), (b) and (c)). In view of the nature of family proceedings the parties and their representatives should act in a conciliatory and constructive manner at all times.

Pre-action procedures for Trusts of Land Act 1996 claims

5.4 For Trusts of Land Act 1996 claims, solicitors (or unrepresented parties) should comply with the following key elements for pre-action procedure, if appropriate, unless there are good reasons for not doing so. These have been adapted from the protocols used in personal injury and clinical negligence cases. They should:

(1) Send an initial letter (referred to in the Civil Procedure Rules 1998 as a 'letter of claim') setting out the following information in concise form:

   (a) a clear summary of uncontroversial facts;
   (b) the main allegations of fact including, where appropriate, a summary of what was said by the parties at the time;
   (c) an indication of the exact financial claim;
   (d) indications as to witnesses and a summary of their evidence;
   (e) disclosure of relevant documents.

Care should be exercised to ensure that the tone of the letter is non-threatening and sets out facts in a non-aggressive way. If addressed to a party who is not represented the letter must advise the party to seek legal advice.

(2) If possible and appropriate, refrain from issuing proceedings for six weeks, during which time full disclosure should be given and negotiations commenced.

(3) Give a preliminary reply within two weeks of receiving the initial letter (letter of claim).

(4) Give a full reply within four weeks of receiving the letter of claim.

5.5 Preparation of the initial letter (letter of claim) will involve a substantial financial commitment from clients. Solicitors must give proper advice to ensure that the claim is framed in the correct way.

5.6 Solicitors must consider and discuss with clients the fact that failure to comply with a pre-action protocol may lead to an order for indemnity costs and other financial penalties.

5.7 Solicitors must consider with clients whether the immediate issue of proceedings is required in order to obtain protection of assets.

5.8 If matters between the parties are concluded without the issue of court proceedings, the outcome should be recorded in a deed.

6   FINANCIAL ISSUES RELATING TO CHILDREN

Private law proceedings relating to children

6.1 Proceedings relating to children will be brought under the Children Act 1989, including proceedings under Schedule 1 for financial provision for children. These proceedings will be subject to guidance under the Private Law Children Protocol (see Part III).

Pre-application protocol for claims under the Children Act 1989, Schedule 1

6.2 Financial claims under Schedule 1 of the Children Act 1989 have no specific pre-application protocol. Nonetheless, many aspects which are relevant to such claims and which should be followed are dealt with in the Pre-application Protocol for Ancillary Relief (see Part IV above).

Applications under Schedule 1 of the Children Act 1989

6.3 As the procedural rules for applications under the Children Act 1989 are not designed primarily for financial applications, solicitors should consider whether there is a need for more disclosure than the standard forms allow. In cases where the standard statement of means might not be sufficient, solicitors should consider applying for a direction allowing service of a detailed questionnaire or use of Form E. Solicitors should also consider, in more complex cases, whether to apply for a direction that a number of the rules of the ancillary relief procedure should apply, particularly in relation to:

(a)   statements of apparent issues;

(b)   chronologies; and

(c)   cost estimates.

6.4 It is good practice to provide costs estimates and solicitors should do so in Children Act 1989, Schedule 1 cases.

6.5 When dealing with final orders, if a property is to be held on trust, careful consideration should be given to who the trustees will be and, where professional trustees are appointed, whether they expect payment and how they might be paid, especially if there is an ongoing trust.

Jurisdiction and in which court to commence proceedings

6.6 Before proceedings relating to disputes about property, money, other belongings and children are issued, solicitors must consider carefully where they should issue the application. Where proceedings about different issues are being conducted in relation to the same couple, all proceedings must, where possible, be heard in the same court. The County Court has unlimited jurisdiction under the Trusts of Land Act 1996 but solicitors should refer to the Civil Procedure Rules 1998, Part 7.2 and the Practice Direction supplementing that (particularly section 2).

6.7 Solicitors should be aware that proceedings may not be started in the High Court unless the value of the claim is more than £15,000 but that if the financial value of the claim, the amount in dispute and/or the complexity of the facts, legal issues, remedies or procedures involved and/or the importance of the outcome of the claim to the public in general are such that claimants and their solicitors believe that their claims ought to be dealt with by a High Court judge, then the case should be issued in the High Court.

PART VI

Domestic abuse

Solicitors should keep under review at all times the availability of public funding and the need to provide clients with costs information at the outset and on a regular basis.

BEFORE THE ISSUE OF AN APPLICATION

1 WHAT IS DOMESTIC ABUSE?

1.1 Domestic abuse has not been defined in English legislation and is decided in any given case on the evidence presented to the court. The following definition, which relies heavily on the definition in the New Zealand Domestic Violence Act 1995, is gender neutral. It has been recommended by the Advisory Board on Family Law in their report to the Lord Chancellor on parental contact in cases where there is domestic violence as the broad definition which should be adopted by the courts.

1.2 Domestic abuse is violence against a person by any other person with whom that person is, or has been, in a domestic relationship.

1.3 Domestic abuse can include:

(a) physical abuse, including slapping, pushing and physical intimidation generally;

(b) sexual abuse;

(c) psychological abuse, including but not limited to –

      (i)   intimidation;

      (ii)   harassment;

      (iii)   damage to property;

      (iv)   threats of physical, sexual or psychological abuse;

  (d)   in relation to a child, causing them to witness or putting them at risk of witnessing the abuse of a person with whom they have a domestic relationship (this does not apply to the person who suffers the abuse).

1.4   Domestic abuse may be a single act or a number of acts forming a pattern of behaviour, even though some or all of these acts when viewed in isolation may appear to be minor or trivial.

2   SCREENING FOR DOMESTIC ABUSE

2.1   The role of solicitors in identifying domestic abuse can be invaluable. In order to respond more effectively to domestic abuse solicitors should:

  (a)   recognise that domestic abuse is a serious problem;

  (b)   be sensitive to different needs and experiences of clients from different backgrounds and cultures;

  (c)   ask questions directly and routinely as part of normal interview procedures;

  (d)   not be judgmental;

  (e)   have information about other sources of help and support available within the local area and keep such information up to date including –

      (i)   domestic violence units at local police stations;

      (ii)   domestic violence liaison officers at police stations if appropriate;

      (iii)   Women's Aid national domestic violence helpline;

      (iv)   women's refuges;

      (v)   Citizens' Advice Bureaux;

      (vi)   Rights of Women;

(vii)   Families Need Fathers;

(viii) support groups;

(ix)   Benefits Agency offices;

(x)   local authority housing departments;

(xi)   local housing trusts;

(xii)   Department of Social Services.

3   SCREENING TECHNIQUES

3.1   Impartial screening techniques should be used as part of normal interview techniques to establish if there is an issue of domestic abuse for that individual client. For example:

(1)   Have you been arguing a lot recently?

(2)   Do you generally have a lot of arguments?

(3)   When you argue, what normally happens?

(4)   Has your partner ever been convicted of any criminal offence, in particular those including violence and/or drugs or alcohol?

(5)   When your partner loses their temper what happens?

(6)   When you or your partner drink alcohol does this ever result in arguments?

(7)   Does your partner ever become violent after consuming alcohol or any other substance?

3.2   If domestic abuse is a suspected issue, more direct questions should be considered, for example:

(1)   Has there ever been any violence between you?

(2)   Have either of you been hurt by the other?

(3)   Are you afraid of your partner?

(4)   Have your children ever witnessed any violence between you?

These questions are based on National Family Mediation guidelines for screening for domestic violence in mediation.

3.3 Even where domestic abuse does not emerge as an issue at the initial interview, the possibility of abuse should be kept under review at all times. Many forms of domestic abuse are hidden and not recognised even by clients. Note that these questions are not exhaustive and they do not represent a comprehensive list.

4 NEEDS ASSESSMENT

4.1 If domestic abuse does emerge as an issue solicitors will need, as appropriate, to:

(1) Explain the options available if clients want to take any action. These include:

    (a) noting the incident but taking no other action at that time;

    (b) visiting their GP;

    (c) contacting the police generally to inquire whether they are prepared to bring a prosecution under the Protection from Harassment Act or other criminal legislation;

    (d) instructing solicitors to send a letter to the alleged abuser recording the incident(s) and demanding the cessation of the abuse with an indication of the further action that might or will be taken if it does not cease;

    (e) applying for legal protection from their partners by way of an injunction.

(2) Advise on the strengths and limitations of each remedy in curbing the abuse and the potential impact on the abuser of any possible course of action.

(3) Advise on the prospects of obtaining an order and the merits, implications and costs of the remedies.

(4) Discuss the potential impact of the domestic abuse on any children and the likely effect upon them of any action clients wish to take.

(5) Discuss how partners' abuse will impact on the other legal remedies or proceedings such as divorce, residence, contact and ancillary relief.

(6) Provide information about other agencies and support groups as appropriate.

(7) Give assistance where appropriate and where possible with the practical problems posed by domestic abuse. For example:

    (a) discuss appropriate contact phone numbers and addresses;

    (b) discuss keeping a log of any incidents which arise;

    (c) discuss keeping certain documents in solicitors' offices.

(8) Consider with clients whether it is appropriate to change the numbers of their mobile and home telephones.

(9) Discuss safety planning and if appropriate prepare an action plan for clients (ideally confirmed to the client in writing).

(10) Suggest to clients that they telephone the police when incidents occur and ask the police to log such incidents and give clients the relevant log number.

(11) Suggest to clients that any injury should be recorded at least by photographs and perhaps by a GP compiling a record of safety planning.

5 COMPILING A RECORD OF EVIDENCE

Gathering evidence

5.1 Solicitors should discuss with clients the need to protect existing evidence of violence or harassment and the need to think about gathering evidence in the future. This may include:

    (a) urging clients to visit their GPs to have a record made of any injuries;

(b)   advising clients to obtain photographs of any injuries immediately after any violent episode (preferably with some evidence of the date on which the photographs were taken);

(c)   asking clients for the names and addresses of any witnesses to the violence or harassment and taking statements from them or asking the client to obtain written statements from them;

(d)   encouraging clients to keep a diary or record of events which has been contemporaneously signed and dated.

Personal statements

5.2   Solicitors should consider and discuss with clients the benefits of making personal statements and, where appropriate, assist clients to do so. A personal statement is a short document, possibly in letter form, setting out a client's statement of the domestic abuse which they state they have suffered. This can be used to provide information to other agencies from which services or support may be needed, for example the Benefits Agency. Clients should be advised that statements may be given to those agencies and that it may be necessary for them to confirm their position verbally.

5.3   This will avoid the need for the client to tell the same story to a number of different agencies, although further details may be required by those agencies. For the statements to be of use they will need to be regularly updated. Clients should be advised that the confidentiality of such statements cannot be guaranteed.

6   SAFETY PLANNING

6.1   As soon as domestic abuse is revealed as an issue, solicitors should consider the safety of clients and any children and advise clients as to how to protect themselves and their children. The following should be considered.

Confidentiality

6.2   Solicitors should discuss with clients their duty of confidentiality and the opportunity to speak openly without fear of disclosure. However, it is very important to explain clearly the limits of that confidentiality, particularly in relation to the court's powers to order disclosure of information about the whereabouts of a child. It should also be made clear that the duty of confidentiality does not extend to infor-mation about the commission of a crime, including child abduction, or about harm or the threat of harm to a child (for guidance on this see Appendix 5 for contact details of Professional Ethics at the Law Society). Solicitors should also consider the guidance given in Principle 16.02 of *The Guide to the Professional Conduct of Solicitors 1999.*

Keeping clients' whereabouts confidential

6.3   When clients are in hiding from their partners, solicitors should discuss with them the possible dangers of disclosure of their whereabouts once proceedings are issued. Solicitors need to consider carefully whether injunctive relief is appropriate in such circumstances.

6.4   Solicitors should consider ways in which clients' whereabouts can be kept confidential, such as:

    (a)   issuing proceedings in a different location (although it will be necessary to explain to clients that there will be an increase in costs as a result of using agents);

    (b)   asking the court for leave to withhold clients' addresses from documentation;

    (c)   the use of agent solicitors in a different area of the country;

    (d)   constant vigilance about the contents of documents;

    (e)   rules about the posting of letters and documents;

    (f)   the court's powers under s.33 of the Family Law Act 1986 in relation to disclosure of the whereabouts of a child.

7   SOURCES OF FUNDING

7.1   Where clients are not eligible for public funding and are not able to pay privately for the cost of legal advice and obtaining protection, solicitors should provide information about other sources of help, for example:

(a)   Women's Aid (WAFE);

(b)   Citizens' Advice Bureaux;

(c)   Rights of Women;

(d)   Families Need Fathers;

(e)   police proceedings under the Protection from Harassment Act 1997.

For contact details of these organisations see Appendix 5.

8   PROTECTION FROM HARASSMENT ACT 1997

8.1   Solicitors should consider whether applications under the Protection from Harassment Act 1997 are more appropriate for clients than applications under Part IV of the Family Law Act 1996. If so, it is important to liaise with the police. They may support a prosecution in appropriate cases, removing the need for any civil proceedings. If there is sufficient evidence to arrest and charge a perpetrator under the Protection from Harassment Act 1997, on conviction the court can impose a restraining order for an unlimited period of time. However, solicitors should consider the different burden of proof in bringing criminal proceedings under the Protection from Harassment Act 1997 as opposed to civil proceedings either under that Act or under Part IV of the Family Law Act 1996.

AFTER THE ISSUE OF AN APPLICATION

9 SERVICE OF PAPERS

9.1 Solicitors should consider asking the court to post papers for service on respondents to their offices. Solicitors can then serve these documents by post or by some other means. This makes it easier to control service of the papers and advise clients when they may need to leave the house. This is not possible in some circumstances without leave of the court. It should also be noted that in certain cases personal service is an absolute requirement. Solicitors are referred to the SFLA Guide to Good Practice on Service (see Appendix 5 for contact details).

10 LEAVING THE HOME

10.1 If clients are still living with violent partners, solicitors need to discuss whether clients need to leave the house before service of proceedings.

10.2 If so, or if clients are considering leaving the family home in any event, temporarily or permanently, it is important to discuss the implications of this action and the effect it may have on the children including financial aspects.

10.3 Consideration should be given to the tactical advantage of moving out immediately or remaining in the property, bearing in mind any potential ancillary relief claim at a later stage. However, client safety is a priority.

10.4 Solicitors should also discuss with clients the need to take with them irreplaceable and important items such as photographs, legal documents and personal items of monetary or sentimental value. Clients may need to remove some of these items prior to leaving the home themselves.

10.5 Solicitors should discuss the possibility of clients returning home with the police if the police are willing/able to assist.

10.6 Solicitors should, however, warn clients that they should not take joint or similarly classed items or strip the house of contents or behave in any other highly inflammatory manner.

10.7 Solicitors must advise clients that if they leave their children with their partners they must not assume that the children will be returned to them automatically by the court.

11 OTHER PROCEEDINGS AND NEGOTIATIONS

11.1 Where domestic abuse is an issue, great care should be taken to ensure that clients' safety is not compromised by meetings arranged by third parties (for example children and family reporting officers) and that clients are not pressured into face-to-face meetings with their ex-partners for the purposes of door of the court negotiations on, for example, children or financial matters. Safety issues should be raised with CAFCASS officers if they are or become involved. Any safety issues within the confines of the court building should be discussed with court staff in advance. The usher should also be informed of any possible difficulties upon arrival at court and asked that if possible separate rooms be made available for a conference so that the client does not have to have face-to-face contact with the other party prior to entering the court.

12 CHILDREN APPLICATIONS AND LEAVE TO APPLY

12.1 Proceedings are sometimes used as tools for abusers to continue their abuse or harassment. Where applications under the Children Act 1989 are used in this way, an application under s.91(14) of the Act, which forbids further applications without leave of the court, should be considered. Courts grant these orders sparingly and solicitors must be aware that courts can be critical of an early application.

13 INJUNCTIONS

13.1 Solicitors need to ensure that the process of obtaining legal protection for parties who are or have been the victims of domestic violence is as supportive, effective and quick as possible.

13.2 Solicitors should make clients aware of the likelihood of costs orders within family proceedings and, above all, ensure that clients are aware that if publicly funded, the statutory charge could apply to any costs incurred within the injunctive relief proceedings. Solicitors should explain that emergency public funding can be granted using devolved powers but that the client must cooperate in the Legal Services Commission's means assessment. If an emergency certificate is granted, it is important that the client understands that a contribution may be payable and he or she will be liable for all the costs incurred on a private client basis if the certificate is revoked (for non-cooperation in the means assessment, because an offer is not accepted, or because it transpires that the client is not financially eligible).

14 WITH OR WITHOUT NOTICE?

14.1 If injunctive relief is appropriate, whether it is appropriate to make a without notice application should be discussed. The issues to consider are:

(a) whether the client may be in danger if proceedings are issued with notice;

(b) the seriousness of the threat to the client, including whether it is urgent and imminent;

(c) the likelihood of the courts granting a without notice order; and

(d) the concerns of courts with regard to the draconian nature of orders made without notice.

14.2 If clients have taken some time to seek help about a violent incident, particularly careful consideration will need to be given as to whether it is appropriate to apply for a without notice order. The seriousness of a threat should not be dismissed simply because of delay as any delay may not indicate the level of fear which clients may feel. Many victims of domestic violence take some time to report the violence. However, where possible solicitors should make a clear legal judgement about whether the court is likely to grant a without notice order and advise in the particular circumstances. Solicitors advising or acting for publicly funded clients must have regard to the Legal Services Commission Funding Code and the Commission's decision-making guidance.

14.3 Solicitors should bear in mind that occupation orders are rarely granted without notice, unless the respondent is out of occupation already.

14.4 Applicants and respondents should both be advised to remain calm during any court proceedings. In cases where clients fear for their safety and are particularly anxious that their addresses are kept confidential, consideration should be given to the arrangements whereby clients arrive at and leave court and where they are situated while waiting at court.

14.5 Solicitors should be aware of the need to have a complete note of hearing details available on request for any party who has not been present at the hearing (*Re W (ex parte orders)* [2000] 2 FLR 927). Applicants' legal representatives should also ensure that the order as drawn contains a list of all affidavits, witness statements and other evidential material read by the judge.

15 LENGTH OF ORDER

15.1 Solicitors must give careful consideration to the proper duration of any order or power of arrest to ensure that clients have protection over a reasonable period of time. For example, the court should not limit the duration of a non-molestation order only because a power of arrest is linked to that order (see *Re B-J (A Child) (Non-Molestation Order: Power of Arrest)* [2000] 2 FCR 599).

16 POWERS OF ARREST

16.1 The need for a power of arrest to be attached to the order must be carefully considered. The practical effect of attaching a power of arrest to an order and how such orders can be enforced must be explained to clients. Solicitors should remember that on a with notice application the court *must* attach a power of arrest to an order where respondents have used or threatened violence against applicants or a relevant child unless satisfied that they will be adequately protected without one. On a without notice application the court has the *discretion* to attach a power of arrest in the above circumstances, based on whether there is a risk of significant harm.

16.2 Where a power of arrest is attached to an order, the local police must be notified and a copy of the order delivered to them. Ideally, process servers should lodge the copy injunction order with the police immediately following service on the respondent. A receipt from the police station should be obtained whenever possible and kept on file.

16.3 Even where a power of arrest is not attached to an order, if there are concerns about the safety of clients, the local police's domestic violence unit should be notified in case a serious incident should arise. Solicitors must warn clients not to encourage breach of an order where a power of arrest is in force and of the result of doing so.

17 ANCILLARY MATTERS

17.1 Where an occupation order is made under the Family Law Act 1996, consideration should be given to requesting that the court exercise its powers under s.53 and Schedule 7 of the Family Law Act 1996 to transfer tenancies between parties and under s.40 to make orders concerning payment of outgoings relating to the home. Note, however, that these orders are currently unenforceable.

18   CRIMINAL EVIDENCE

18.1   Where alleged perpetrators of domestic abuse have criminal records or there are concurrent criminal proceedings, consideration should be given to introducing findings from these proceedings into the family proceedings in appropriate cases. Where there are concurrent criminal proceedings, solicitors should consider seeking an adjournment of any family proceedings until after the criminal proceedings have been concluded.

19   ACTING FOR THE RESPONDENT

Public funding

19.1   Solicitors should provide the following information to any clients who are respondents in proceedings for injunctions.

(1)   Respondents are unlikely to justify a grant of legal representation unless:

(a)   an application has been made for an occupation order (unless the respondent is already out of occupation of the property, has no good reason to return and any other issues in the proceedings are insufficient to justify public funding being used); and/or

(b)   there are very serious allegations which are denied wholly or substantially; and/or

(c)   there is any question of inability to defend (for example because of mental incapacity or minority).

(2)   Respondents in appropriate cases will be assisted by the availability of 'Help at Court' to advise about the giving of undertakings.

Preparing for court

19.2   When a case is going to court solicitors, or respondents if acting in person, should:

(a)   wherever possible, prepare a statement in reply to applicants' sworn statements in readiness for the hearing wherever possible;

(b)   consider what evidence could be obtained to support the respondent's case, including evidence from the housing department about the likelihood of either party being rehoused if an occupation order is made;

(c)   consider the need for cross-applications for non-molestation and occupation orders, if there are allegations of assault on both sides.

19.3   Where a return date is fixed, the respondent's sworn statement in reply should be filed and served as soon as possible prior to the return date. If possible, any additional evidence should be adduced before the return date. If this is not possible, the applicant's solicitors should be advised in writing of the intention to adduce further evidence and, if necessary, leave should be sought at the return date hearing.

20   AT COURT

20.1   In accordance with para. 14.4 above, applicants and respondents should both be advised of the wisdom of remaining calm during any court proceedings.

20.2   Where possible an application for a non-molestation order should be resolved by giving undertakings (perhaps cross-undertakings). However, as a power of arrest will not attach to an undertaking, solicitors should advise respondents that there is a real possibility that an undertaking will not be accepted for that or another reason, so that clients are not given false hopes or false expectations.

21   OTHER PROCEEDINGS

21.1   Solicitors should consider and advise on the following:

(1)   Whether proceedings need to be launched under the Children Act 1989 if there are concerns about where any child should live or in relation to contact arrangements between the child and their non-resident parent.

(2)   Whether an application for a transfer of a tenancy under Schedule 7 of the Family Law Act 1996 would be appropriate. Where necessary, an order should be sought preventing either party filing a notice to quit which would render both parties homeless. If a tenancy is in joint names and one party surrenders that tenancy for any reason, including vindictiveness, the consequences are that the other party is left homeless and is deemed to have made themselves voluntarily homeless.

22   CONTACT

22.1   If respondents have concerns about contact with any children, this should be raised at the first hearing. If applicants refuse contact, directions can be given and an undertaking given to issue an application at that first hearing (see Appendix 3).

22.2   Solicitors must advise respondents of the importance of regaining the trust of parents with residence where contact is concerned.

23   AFTER THE HEARING

23.1   Solicitors must advise clients in writing of the order that has been made and the consequences of breaching it. In appropriate cases, solicitors should advise clients that any communications with applicants should be dealt with through solicitors because of the risk that any attempt to contact applicants by other means would probably be seen as harassment.

23.2 Once proceedings have been concluded it may be possible for mediation to be considered, notwithstanding that there has been violence within the relationship.

23.3 Solicitors should ensure that clients understand the meanings of orders and should advise parties not to act in such a way that would put the other party at risk of committal proceedings, for example by telephoning a party who is forbidden to contact them.

PART VII

Mediation

Solicitors should keep under review at all times the availability of public funding and the need to provide clients with costs information at the outset and on a regular basis.

1 WHAT IS MEDIATION?

1.1 Family mediation is a process in which:

(a) a couple or any other family members

(b) whether or not they are legally represented

(c) and at any time, whether or not there are or have been legal proceedings

(d) agree to the appointment of a neutral third party (the mediator)

(e) who is impartial

(f) who has no authority to make any decisions with regard to their issues

(g) which may relate to separation, divorce, children's issues, property and financial questions or any other issues that may arise

(i) but who helps them reach their own informed decisions

(j) by negotiation

(k) without adjudication; a mediator should not give advice.

This definition is taken from the Law Society's Code of Practice for solicitors practising as family mediators. This

Code of Practice and the Law Society's Standards are available on written request from the Law Society (see Appendix 5 for contact details). The UK College of Family Mediators has also produced a Code of Practice and Standards available on written request from the UK College of Family Mediators and on the website (see Appendix 5 for contact details). Mediators providing publicly funded mediation must work to the Legal Services Commission's quality assurance standard for mediation, available on their website.

1.2 From time to time the dispute between a couple may involve a wider group of family members than just the couple. Family members may include step-parents, grandparents, aunts, uncles, children and even potential family members. Any of these may participate in the mediation with the agreement of the couple and the mediator (although children do not usually participate directly and can only do so when the mediator is specifically trained to involve children).

2 SCREENING FOR MEDIATION

2.1 It is important that only those cases that are suitable are referred to mediation.

2.2 At an early stage solicitors must, unless it is clearly inappropriate to do so, explain the mediation process and advise clients on the benefits and/or limitations of mediation in their particular case, as well as the role of solicitors in supporting the mediation process.

2.3 Family mediation usually involves both parties meeting with the mediator at the same time. Mediation can resolve issues in dispute or narrow those issues but it may not be appropriate in some circumstances, at least until other steps (for example applying for interim maintenance, a freezing order or obtaining domestic protection) have been put in hand. Mediation would be inappropriate at a time:

(a) where there are child protection issues or a risk of child abduction;

(b) where clients do not have the capacity to mediate or their mental competence is in question;

(c) before emergency procedures which need to be taken have been concluded;

(d) where a particular issue can only be adjudicated upon by the court, for example, in paternity cases;

(e) in financial proceedings where either party is bankrupt;

(f) where bail conditions are in place restricting one party having contact with the other party.

2.4 Mediation may also not be appropriate in the following circumstances:

(1) Where domestic abuse has occurred or is still occurring. If clients still want to mediate in such cases, the risks should be discussed and whether any action can be taken to make them feel safe in the mediation. The term domestic abuse is defined in Part VI and guidance is given on screening, safety planning, etc.

(2) Where the imbalance between parties is likely to be beyond the capacities of mediators to address, although solicitors should be aware of the need to consider mediation in certain publicly funded cases.

(3) Where reconciliation may be possible and counselling or marital therapy may be more appropriate at this stage.

This is not an all-inclusive list but covers most situations which are unsuitable for mediation.

3   WHICH MEDIATOR?

3.1 Solicitors who refer clients to mediation should provide details of mediators who have undertaken appropriate training and have obtained accreditation with an established organisation. These details should be kept up to date.

3.2 Solicitors should advise publicly funded clients on the availability of publicly funded mediation and that the statutory charge does not apply to work done in respect of mediation.

4 THE BENEFITS OF MEDIATION

4.1 Solicitors should explain to their clients the potential benefits of mediation. These include:

(1) When parties divorce or separate, it is generally better if both parties can sort out together the practical arrangements for the future.

(2) The aim of mediation is to help parties find a solution that meets the needs of all involved, especially the children, and that both parties feel is fair. At the end of mediation, those involved should feel that there has been no 'winner or loser' but that together they have arrived at sensible, workable arrangements.

(3) Mediation can help to reduce tension, hostility and misunderstandings and so improve communication between parties. This is especially important if children are involved as parties may need to co-operate over their care and upbringing for some years to come.

(4) Mediation has economic benefits because if a party is eligible for publicly funded family mediation they will not be required to make any contribution towards the cost of the mediation. If a party is eligible for mediation then they will also be eligible for legal advice in respect of that mediation during and at the end of the mediation and they will not need to make a contribution to this.

5 THE TIMING OF THE REFERRAL TO MEDIATION

5.1 It is important that solicitors should carefully consider and advise as to the timing of any referral to mediation. In publicly funded cases there is a requirement to consider mediation at the commencement of the matter and before a full certificate can be obtained. However, even if the case is unsuitable for mediation at the outset, the possibility of a later referral should be kept under review as funding could be available for such a later referral. In private matters the timing of the referral is a matter for careful consideration, depending on the facts of the case. For example, it may be appropriate to refer contact disputes to mediation early on. On financial matters it may sometimes be appropriate to deal with disclosure prior to such referral.

6 SUPPORTING CLIENTS IN MEDIATION

6.1 It is accepted that mediation works best when supported by independent legal advice. When referring clients to mediation solicitors should explain that:

(a) the mediation process should be supported by independent legal advice;

(b) public funding is available for this by way of 'Help with Mediation';

(c) any financial agreement is not directly binding between the parties until it has been approved by the court as a consent order (and the importance of this);

(d) parties may consult their solicitors at any stage in mediation but this is particularly important when disclosure and settlement proposals are being considered; and

(e) seeking advice from solicitors between mediation sessions can be positively helpful in seeing whether proposals are appropriate.

7 THE ROLE OF SOLICITORS DURING MEDIATION

7.1 The role of solicitors during the mediation process is very important. When clients are going through mediation solicitors should:

(a) assist clients to provide disclosure where necessary and assess the disclosure which takes place in mediation (use of a Form E as a standard for disclosure in mediation is recommended as it has been adopted for use in mediation and has been approved by the mediation bodies and the LCD);

(b) give advice about settlement proposals as and when required, bearing in mind the long-term interests of clients and/or any children;

(c) give advice about other options;

(d) bear in mind the cost of mediation as opposed to negotiation through solicitors or court proceedings;

(e) give advice about any untenable position either clients or their partners may be adopting;

(f) assist clients to reach a decision and encourage clients to raise issues in mediation as appropriate.

8 THE ROLE OF SOLICITORS FOLLOWING MEDIATION

8.1 Proposals made in mediation are not binding between the parties. It is very important that the parties have access to independent legal advice when proposals are made.

8.2 Following mediation, where the client has reached no firm proposals the solicitor should:

(a) discuss the reasons for the discontinuation of the mediation;

(b) note what has been achieved; and

(c) discuss the options.

8.3 Where the parties have produced interim proposals, discuss the position and any potential difficulties, including the need to apply for any interim orders.

8.4 Where proposals have been made, follow the guidance in the main protocol (see Part I, paras. 5.1–5.4) and where it is appropriate to draft a consent order dealing with finances, the guidance on consent orders should be followed (see Part IV, paras. 16.1–16.6).

Practice Direction (Family Proceedings: Court Bundles)

INTRODUCTION

Solicitors need to comply with the President's Practice Direction on Court Bundles of 10 March 2000, which is reproduced below (*Practice Direction (Family Proceedings: Court Bundles)* [2000] 1 FLR 536).

Solicitors must note that

(1)   The Practice Direction applies to:

(a)   all hearings in the Royal Courts of Justice with any time estimate;

(b)   to any hearing with a time estimate of half a day or more in all care centres, family hearing centres and divorce county courts (including the Principal Registry where it is treated as a divorce county court).

(2)   It is good practice, in complex cases, or where the documentation is voluminous, for the parties to agree an essential reading list for the judge and lodge it at the commencement of the bundle, with the other documents required by paragraph 3.1 of the Practice Direction (*Re CH (A Minor)* [1998] 1FLR 402.)

PRESIDENT'S PRACTICE DIRECTION ON COURT BUNDLES (10 MARCH 2000)

1.   The following practice applies to all hearings in family proceedings in the High Court, to all hearings of family proceedings in the Royal Courts of Justice and to hearings with a time estimate of half a day or more in all care centres, family hearing centres and divorce county courts (including the Principal Registry of the Family Division when so treated), except as specified in paragraph 2.3 below, and subject to specific directions given in any particular case. 'Hearing' extends to

all hearings before judges and district judges and includes the hearing of any application.

2.1   A bundle for the use of the court at the hearing shall be provided by the party in the position of applicant at the hearing or by any other party who agrees to do so. It shall contain copies of all documents relevant to the hearing in chronological order, paginated and indexed and divided into separate sections, as follows:

(a)   applications and orders;

(b)   statements and affidavits;

(c)   experts' reports and other reports including those of a guardian ad litem;

(d)   other documents, divided into further sections as may be appropriate.

2.2   Where the nature of the hearing is such that a complete bundle of all documents is unnecessary, the bundle may comprise only those documents necessary for the hearing but the summary (see paragraph 3.1(a) below) must commence with a statement that the bundle is limited or incomplete. The summary should be limited to those matters which the court needs to know for the purpose of the hearing and for management of the case.

2.3   The requirement to provide a bundle shall not apply to the hearing of any urgent application where the circumstances are such that it is not reasonably practicable for a bundle to be provided.

3.1   At the commencement of the bundle there shall be:

(a)   a summary of the background to the hearing limited, if practicable, to one A4 page;

(b)   a statement of the issue or issues to be determined;

(c)   a summary of the order or directions sought by each party;

(d)   a chronology if it is a final hearing or if the summary under (a) is insufficient;

(e)   skeleton arguments as may be appropriate with copies of all authorities relied on.

3.2   If possible the bundle shall be agreed. In all cases, the party preparing the bundle shall paginate it and provide an index to all other parties prior to the hearing.

3.3   The bundle should normally be contained in a ring binder or lever arch file (limited to 350pp in each file). Where there is more than one bundle, each should be clearly distinguishable. Bundles shall be lodged, if practicable, two clear days prior to the hearing. For hearings in the Royal Courts of Justice bundles shall be lodged with the

Clerk of the Rules. All bundles shall have clearly marked on the out-side, the title and number of the case, the hearing date and time and, if known, the name of the judge hearing the case.

4. After each hearing which is not a final hearing, the party responsible for the bundle shall retrieve it from the court. The bundle with any additional documents shall be re-lodged for further hearings in accordance with the above provisions.

5. This direction replaces paragraphs (5) and (8) of *Practice Direction: Case Management (31 January 1995)* [1995] 1 FLR 456 and shall have effect from 2 May 2000.

Issued with the approval and concurrence of the Lord Chancellor.

SFLA's Code of Conduct

INTRODUCTION: CODE OF PRACTICE FOR SFLA MEMBERS

SFLA solicitors believe in using an approach which is sensitive, constructive, cost-effective and most likely to result in an agreement. To achieve this, SFLA members follow this Code of Practice.

The Association was created in 1982 when there was widespread concern that solicitors and court procedures were adding to the distress and anger that can arise when family relationships break down. Our members believe that solicitors should deal with matters in a way designed to preserve people's dignity and encourage them to reach agreement. The result will often be to achieve the same or more satisfactory solutions than going to court but at less cost – in terms of emotion and money.

Most importantly, this approach is more likely to encourage family members to deal with each other in a civilised way. For example, it helps parents to put their own differences aside and to agree arrangements that are best for their children. Experience shows that agreed solutions are more likely to work in the long term than arrangements imposed by a court. Even when proceedings are necessary, it is best for the whole family if the proceedings are conducted in a constructive and realistic way rather than as if in the midst of a war zone.

WHAT IS THE SFLA?

- We are an association of over [5,000] solicitors who agree to follow this Code of Practice. The Law Society recommends that all solicitors practising family law should follow this Code. Our members should explain the Code to their clients, as it will form the basis of the approach that they adopt.

- We are actively involved in law reform, both initiating improvements and responding to proposals for change.

- We provide education for our members to equip them to deal with both the legal and practical issues of family breakdown and its emotional consequences. We encourage mediation and counselling where appropriate.

- Our members vary from newly-qualified solicitors to those with many years of experience. However, membership is not a guarantee of excellence or legal ability.

- We produce guidance on good practice in specific areas of family law work.

- Keeping to the Code is not a sign of weakness. It does not expose the client to disadvantage. The approach the solicitor adopts should be firm and fair. Solicitors are not prevented from taking immediate and decisive action where necessary. Even when there are ongoing discussions, court proceedings may be started and continue at the same time in case negotiations do not produce an agreement.

- The Code is not a straightjacket. Its guidelines cannot be absolute rules. It may be necessary to depart from the Code if professional rules or duties require it.

GENERAL

(1) At an early stage, you should explain to your client the approach you adopt in family law work.

(2) You should encourage your client to see the advantages to the family of a constructive and non-confrontational approach as a way of resolving differences. You should advise, negotiate and conduct matters so as to help the family members settle their differences as quickly as possible and reach agreement, while allowing them time to reflect, consider and come to terms with their new situation.

(3) You should make sure that your client understands that the best interests of the child should be put first. You should explain that where a child is involved, your client's attitude to the other family members will affect the family as a whole and the child's relationship with his or her parents.

(4) You should encourage the attitude that a family dispute is not a contest in which there is a winner and a loser, but rather that it is a search for fair solutions. You should avoid using words or phrases that suggest or cause a dispute when there is no serious dispute.

(5) Emotions are often intense in family disputes. You should avoid inflaming them in any way.

(6) You should take great care when considering the effect your correspondence could have on other family members and your own client. Your letters should be clearly understandable and free of jargon. Remember that clients may see assertive letters between solicitors as aggressive declarations of war. Your correspondence should aim to resolve issues and to settle the matter, not to further inflame

emotions or to antagonise. You should not express your personal opinions on the behaviour of your client's husband or wife.

(7)   You should stress the need for your client to be open and honest in all aspects of the case. You must explain what could happen if your client is not open and honest.

RELATIONSHIP WITH A CLIENT

(8)   You should make sure that you are objective and do not allow your own emotions or personal opinions to influence your advice.

(9)   You must give advice and explain all options to your client. The client must understand the consequences of any decisions they have to make. The decision is to be made by your client; you cannot decide for your client.

(10)   You must make your client aware of the legal costs at all stages. The benefits and merits of any step must be balanced against the costs.

(11)   You should make sure that your client knows about other available services (such as mediation and counselling) which may bring about a settlement, help your client, the possibility of a reconciliation and, where appropriate, give every encouragement.

DEALING WITH OTHER SOLICITORS

(12)   In all dealings with other solicitors, you should show courtesy and try to maintain a good working relationship.

(13)   You should try to avoid criticising the other solicitors involved in a case.

DEALING WITH A PERSON WHO DOES NOT HAVE A SOLICITOR

(14)   When you are dealing with someone who is not represented by a solicitor, you should take even greater care to communicate clearly and try to avoid any technical language or jargon which is not easily understood.

(15)   You should strongly recommend an unrepresented person to consult an SFLA solicitor in the interests of the family.

COURT PROCEEDINGS

(16)   When taking any step in the proceedings, the long-term effect on your client and other family members must be balanced with the likely short-term benefit to the case.

(17)   If the purpose of taking a particular step in proceedings may be misunderstood or appear hostile, you should consider explaining it, as soon as possible, to the others involved in the case.

(18)   Before filing a petition, you and your client should consider whether the other party or his or her solicitor should be contacted in advance about the petition, the 'facts' on which the petition is to be based and the particulars, with a view to coming to an agreement and minimising misunderstanding.

(19)   When you or your client receive a Petition or Statement of Arrangements for approval, unless there are exceptional circumstances, you should advise your client not to start their own proceedings without giving the other party at least seven days' notice, in writing, of the intention to do so.

(20)   You should discourage your client from naming a co-respondent unless there are very good reasons to do so.

CHILDREN

(21)   You should encourage both your client and other family members to put the child's welfare first.

(22)   You should encourage parents to co-operate when making decisions concerning the child, and advise parents that it is often better to make arrangements for the child between themselves, through their solicitors or through a mediator rather than through a court hearing.

(23)   In any letters you write, you should keep disputes about arrangements for the child separate from disputes about money. They should usually be referred to in separate letters.

(24)   You must remember that the interests of the child may not reflect those of either parent. In exceptional cases it may be appropriate for the child to be represented separately by the Official Solicitor, a panel guardian (in Specified proceedings) or, in the case of a 'mature' child, by another solicitor.

WHEN THE CLIENT IS A CHILD

(25)   You should only accept instructions from a child if you have the necessary training and expertise in this field.

(26) You must continually assess the child's ability to give instructions.

(27) You should make sure that the child has enough information to make informed decisions. The solicitor should advise and give information in a clear and understandable way and be aware that certain information may be harmful to the child.

(28) You should not show favour towards either parent, the local authority or any other person involved in the court proceedings.

(29) Detailed guidelines for solicitors acting for children have been drawn up by the SFLA. Copies are available from Mary I'Anson, Administrative Director, SFLA, PO Box 302, Orpington, BR6 8QX.

If you would like a list of local SFLA members, please send a stamped addressed envelope to the SFLA office, address above.

CASC guidelines for good practice (parental contact in cases of domestic violence)

THE ADVISORY BOARD ON FAMILY LAW: CHILDREN ACT SUB-COMMITTEE GUIDELINES FOR GOOD PRACTICE ON PARENTAL CONTACT IN CASES WHERE THERE IS DOMESTIC VIOLENCE

This is an extract from section 5 of the Report of the Children Act Sub-Committee to the Lord Chancellor on the question of parental contact in cases where there is domestic violence.

Court to give early consideration to allegations of domestic violence

1.1 In every case in which domestic violence is put forward as a reason for refusing or limiting contact the court should at the earliest opportunity consider the allegations made (and any answer to them) and decide whether the nature and effect of the violence alleged by the complainant (or admitted by the respondent) is such as to make it likely that the order of the court for contact will be affected if the allegations are proved.

Steps to be taken where the court forms the view that its order is likely to be affected if allegations of domestic violence are proved

1.2 Where the allegations are disputed and the court forms the view that the nature and effect of the violence alleged is such as to make it likely that the order of the court will be affected if the allegations are proved the court should:

    (a)   consider what evidence will be required to enable the court to make findings of fact in relation to the allegations;

(b)   ensure that appropriate directions under s.11(1) of the Children Act 1989 are given at an early stage in the application to enable the matters in issue to be heard as speedily as possible; including consideration of whether or not it would be appropriate for there to be an initial hearing for the purpose of enabling findings of fact to be made;

(c)   consider whether an order for interim contact pending the final hearing is in the interests of the child; and in particular that the safety of the child and the residential parent can be secured before during and after any such contact;

(d)   direct a report from a children and family reporter on the question of contact unless satisfied that it is not necessary to do so in order to safeguard the child's interests;

(e)   subject to the seriousness of the allegations made and the difficulty of the case consider whether or not the children in question need to be separately represented in the proceedings; and, if the case is proceeding in the Family Proceedings Court whether or not it should be transferred to the County Court; if in the County Court whether or not it should be transferred to the High Court for hearing.

Directions to the Children and Family Reporter in cases involving domestic violence

1.3   (a)   Where the court orders a welfare report under s.7 of the Children Act 1989 in a disputed application for contact in which it considers domestic violence to be a relevant issue, the order of the court should contain specific directions to the children and family reporter to address the issue of domestic violence; to make an assessment of the harm which the children have suffered or which they are at risk of suffering if contact is ordered; to assess whether the safety of the child and the residential parent can be secured before, during and after contact; and to make particular efforts to ascertain the wishes and feelings of the children concerned in the light of the allegations of violence made.

(b)   Where the court has made findings of fact prior to the children and family reporter conducting his or her investigation, the court should ensure that either a note of the court's judgment or of the findings of fact made by the court is made available to the children and family reporter as soon after the findings have been made as is practicable.

(c)   Where in a case involving allegations of domestic violence the whereabouts of the child and the residential parent are known to the court but not known to the parent seeking contact; and where the court takes the view that it is in the best interests of the child or children concerned for that position to be maintained for the time being, the court should give directions designed to ensure that any welfare report on the circumstances of the residential parent and the child does not reveal their whereabouts, whether directly or indirectly.

Interim contact pending a full hearing

1.4 In deciding any question of interim contact pending a full hearing the court should:

(a) specifically take into account the matters set out in s.1(3) of the Children Act 1989 ('the welfare check-list');

(b) give particular consideration to the likely risk of harm to the child, whether physical and/or emotional, if contact is either granted or refused;

(c) consider, if it decides such contact is in the interests of the child, what directions are required about how it is to be carried into effect; and, in particular, whether it should be supervised, and if so, by whom; and generally, in so far as it can, ensure that any risk of harm to the child is minimised and the safety of the child and residential parent before during and after any such contact is secured;

(d) consider whether it should exercise its powers under s.42(2)(B) of the Family Law Act 1996 to make a non-molestation order;

(e) consider whether the parent seeking contact should seek advice and/or treatment as a precondition to contact being ordered or as a means of assisting the court in ascertaining the likely risk of harm to the child from that person at the final hearing.

Matters to be considered at the final hearing

1.5 At the final hearing of a contact application in which there are disputed allegations of domestic violence:

(a) the court should, wherever practicable, make findings of fact as to the nature and degree of the violence which is established on the balance of probabilities and its effect on the child and the parent with whom the child is living;

(b) in deciding the issue of contact the court should, in the light of the findings of fact which it has made, apply the individual items in the welfare checklist with reference to those findings; in particular, where relevant findings of domestic violence have been made, the court should in every case consider the harm which the child has suffered as a consequence of that violence and the harm which the child is at risk of suffering if an order for contact is made and only make an order for contact if it can be satisfied that the safety of the residential parent and the child can be secured before during and after contact.

Matters to be considered where findings of domestic violence are made

1.6 In each case where a finding of domestic violence is made, the court should consider the conduct of both parents towards each other and towards the children; in particular, the court should consider:

(a) the effect of the domestic violence which has been established on the child and on the parent with whom the child is living;

(b) whether or not the motivation of the parent seeking contact is a desire to promote the best interests of the child or as a means of continuing a process of violence against or intimidation or harassment of the other parent;

(c) the likely behaviour of the parent seeking contact during contact and its effect on the child or children concerned;

(d) the capacity of the parent seeking contact to appreciate the effect of past and future violence on the other parent and the children concerned;

(e) the attitude of the parent seeking contact to past violent conduct by that parent; and in particular whether that parent has the capacity to change and/or to behave appropriately.

Matters to be considered where contact is ordered in a case where findings of domestic violence have been made

1.7 Where the court has made findings of domestic violence but, having applied the welfare checklist, nonetheless considers that direct contact is in the best interests of the child or children concerned, the court should consider (in addition to the matters set out in paragraphs 5 and 6 above) what directions are required to enable the order to be carried into effect under s.11(7) of the Children Act 1989 and in particular should consider:

(a) whether or not contact should be supervised, and if so, by whom;

(b) what conditions (for example by way of seeking advice or treatment) should be complied with by the party in whose favour the order for contact has been made;

(c)   whether the court should exercise its powers under s.42(2)(B) of the Family Law Act 1996 to make a non-molestation order;

(d)   whether such contact should be for a specified period or should contain provisions which are to have effect for a specified period;

(e)   setting a date for the order to be reviewed and giving directions to ensure that the court at the review has full information about the operation of the order.

Information about local facilities

1.8   The court should also take steps to inform itself (alternatively direct the children and family reporter or the parties to inform it) of the facilities available locally to the court to assist parents who have been violent to their partners and/or their children, and, where appropriate, should impose as a condition of future contact that violent parents avail themselves of those facilities.

Reasons

1.9   In its judgement or reasons the court should always explain how its findings on the issue of domestic violence have influenced its decision on the issue of contact; and in particular where the court has found domestic violence proved but nonetheless makes an order for contact, the court should always explain, whether by way of reference to the welfare check-list or otherwise why it takes the view that contact is in the best interests of the child.

Note

1.10   Although not part of our formal guidelines, we think that all courts hearing applications where domestic violence is alleged should review their facilities at court and should do their best to ensure that there are separate waiting areas for the parties in such cases and that information about the services of Victim Support and other supporting agencies is readily available.

Background Information

●   The Report and Guidelines were published over Easter 2000.
●   The Guidelines were referred to by the Court of Appeal in the Judgment in *Re: L (A Child) and Others,* handed down on the 19 June 2000.

- On 6 March 2001 Jane Kennedy, Parliamentary Secretary in the Lord Chancellor's Department, announced in the House of Commons that the government endorsed the report of the Children Act Sub-Committee entitled 'Parental Contact in Cases where there is Domestic Violence', and the Guidelines for Good Practice. Ms Kennedy also outlined that the government will work in partnership with the President of the Family Division to ensure the widest promulgation of the Guidelines, will work in partnership with the sub-committee to monitor the effectiveness of the Guidelines, and that at the end of the monitoring period will consider the need for amending legislation in the light of that monitoring.

- The report uses the term *court welfare officer*. This term has since been amended by the Family Proceedings (Amendment) Rules 2001 [SI 2001/821] and the Family Proceedings Courts (Children Act 1989) (Amendment) Rules 2001 [SI 2001/818] to *children and family reporter*. The terms *court welfare officer's report* and *welfare officer's report* have now been replaced by *welfare report*. This document reflects those changes.

Family Policy Division
Lord Chancellor's Department
April 2001

NACCC protocol for referrals of families by judges and magistrates to child contact centres

This protocol has been designed to assist judges and magistrates who are proposing to make orders for contact involving the use of a Child Contact Centre. It has the endorsement of The Rt. Hon. Dame Elizabeth Butler-Sloss, D.B.E. and Mr. Justice Wall.

Before making an order for contact (whether interim or final) which involves the use of a Child Contact Centre, please check that the matters listed below have been addressed.

Please note in particular that most Child Contact Centres do not offer supervised contact. The provision which most offer is supported contact which is described in the *Manual of Guidance* produced by the National Association of Child Contact Centres (NACCC) as:

- low vigilance;
- several families at a time in one or a number of rooms;
- volunteers and staff keeping a watchful eye;
- conversations not being monitored.

If you are considering making an order for contact in a case where domestic violence is an issue please ensure that you have addressed that issue, and in particular:

1. That you have considered the effect on the resident parent and the children concerned of any domestic violence which you have found or which is alleged and that;

2. Notwithstanding these matters you are satisfied that supported contact is appropriate is appropriate. If it is not appropriate is supervised contact appropriate and is it available?

Things to check:

1. That the child contact centre co-ordinator has been contacted and has confirmed

(a) The referral appears to be suitable for that particular centre. Child contact centres can refuse to accept families if the circumstances appear inappropriate for the centre.

(b) The intended day and times are available at the particular centre concerned.

(c) A vacancy is available or a place on the waiting list has been allocated.

2. That you have directed that a copy of the order is provided to the centre by one or other of the parties within a specified time together with any other injunctive or relevant orders on the court file.

3. That it has been agreed who will have the responsibility for completing and returning the centre's referral form. Solicitors for both parties should agree the contents and it should be forwarded to the child contact centre within 24 hours of the court hearing.

4. If contact is to be observed at the child contact centre by a CAFCASS officer or other third party that this is a facility offered by that centre and that the centre has agreed to this course of action. (Many do not permit such attendance.)

5. That the parties understand whether the centre offers supported or supervised contact and appreciate the difference.

6. That it is agreed who is going to tell the children where and when they will see their non-resident parent.

7. That the order clearly defines whether or not other family members are to be a part of the contact visit.

8. That it has been agreed who will be responsible for informing the centre when the place is no longer required.

9. That a date has been set for a review of the contact and any other steps the parties have been ordered or undertaken to take which are relevant to the contact issue and for further directions if necessary. Only in exceptional circumstances should use of a centre be open-ended.

Please also note:

1. The order should be worded 'Subject to the parties' attendance at a pre-contract meeting (if applicable), the availability of a place and the parties abiding by the rules of the centre . . .'

   Note: It is a requirement of some centres that the parents and children attend a pre-contact meeting (parents are seen separately) so that the centres can follow their own risk assessment procedure. Others will welcome or insist on a pre-contact visit by the resident parent to acclimatise the child(ren). Non-resident parents are also welcome.

2.   *Ben's Story*, a children's book about visiting a child contact centre is available from NACCC or can be ordered from bookshops. It is also printed in Welsh.

3.   The centre or centres at which you direct contact to take place will very much welcome a visit from you or from your colleagues. It will be greatly appreciated by the volunteer staff if the local judiciary takes an interest in its local centres and such visits will help you to understand the facilities on offer and thus the type of case which is most suited to contact in the local child contact centre.

APPENDIX 5

Useful contacts and addresses

The Abduction Unit
Lord Chancellor's Department
81 Chancery Lane
London WC2A 1DD
Tel: 020 7911 7047/7045
Fax: 020 7911 7248
E-mail: *enquiries@offsol.gsi.gov.uk*

Association of Child Abuse
Lawyers
PO Box 466
Chorleywood
Rickmansworth, Herts
WD3 5LG
Tel: 01923 286888
E-mail: *leemoore@aol.com*
www.abny.demon.co.uk

Association of Lawyers for
Children (ALC)
60 Wyndham Street
Barry
Vale of Glamorgan
CF63 4EL
Tel: 01446 746973
E-mail: *admin@alc.org.uk*
www.alc.org.uk

CAFCASS Headquarters
6th Floor
16 Palace Street
London
SW1E 5LX
Tel: 020 7210 4420
Fax: 020 7210 4422
E-mail: *cafcass@cafcass.gov.uk*

Child Support Agency
Headquarters
Office of the Chief Executive
CSA Room 158A
Benton Park Road
Newcastle
NE98 1YX
Tel: 08457 133133 (National
Helpline)
www.dss.gov.uk/csa

The Court Service
Southside
105 Victoria Street
London SW1E 6QT
Tel: 020 7210 2266
www.courtservice.gov.uk

Families Need Fathers
134 Curtain Road
London
EC2A 3AR
Tel: 020 7613 5060
E-mail: *fnf@fnf.orf.uk*

The Law Society (general enquiries)
113 Chancery Lane
London WC2A 1PL
Tel: 020 7242 1222
DX: 56 London/Chancery Lane
www.lawsociety.org.uk

Law Society's Child Panel
(Information Pack)
The Law Society
Ipsley Court
Berrington Close
Redditch
Worcs B98 OTD
Tel: 0870 606 2555

Law Society's Family Law Panel
(Information Pack)
The Law Society
Ipsley Court
Berrington Close
Redditch
Worcs B98 0TD
Tel: 0870 606 2555

Law Society's Family Mediation
Panel (Information Pack)
The Law Society
Ipsley Court
Berrington Close
Redditch
Worcs B98 OTD
Tel: 0870 606 2555

Legal Services Commission (LSC)
85 Gray's Inn Road
London
WC1X 8AA
Tel: 020 7759 0000
www.legalservices.gov.uk

National Association of Child
Contact Centres (NACCC)
Minerva House
Spaniel Row
Nottingham
NG1 6EP
Tel: 0870 7703269
E-mail: *contact@naccc.org.uk*

National Association of Citizen's
Advice Bureaux (NACAB)
115–123 Pentonville Road
London
N1 9LZ
Tel: 020 7833 2181

National Association of Guardian
ad Litems and Reporting Officers
(NAGALRO)
PO Box 264
Esher
Surrey KT10 0WA
Tel: 01372 818504
www.nagalro.com

National Family and Parenting
Institute
430 Highgate Studios
53–70 Highate Road
London
NW5 1TL
Tel: 020 74243460
Fax: 020 74853590
E-mail: *info@nfpi.org.uk*

National Council for One Parent
Families
255 Kentish Town Road
London
NW5 2LX
Telephone: 020 7428 5400
Fax: 020 7482 4851
E-mail:
info@oneparentfamilies.org.uk

Office of the Official Solicitor and
Public Trustee
81 Chancery Lane
London WC2A 1DD
Tel: 020 7911 7127
E-mail: *enquiries@offsol.gsi.gov.uk*

Professional Ethics
The Law Society
Ipsley Court
Redditch
Worcs B98 0TD
Tel: 0870 606 2577

Relate
Herbert Gray College
Little Church Street
Rugby, Warwickshire
CV21 3AP
Tel: 01788 573241
Fax: 01788 535007
www.relate.org.uk

Rights of Women
52–54 Featherstone Street
London
EC1Y 8RT
Advice line: 020 7251 6577

Solicitors Family Law Association
(SFLA)
PO Box 302
Orpington, Kent
BR6 8QX
Tel: 01689 850227
Fax: 01689 855833
DX: 86853 Locksbottom
E-mail: *mary.ianson@sfla.org.uk*

UK College of Family Mediators
24–32 Stephenson Way
London
NW1 2HX
Tel: 020 7391 9162
Fax: 020 7391 9165
www.ukcfm.co.uk

Women's Aid Federation of
England
PO Box 391
Bristol
BS99 7WS
Tel: 0117 944 4411
Fax: 0117 9241703
Helpline: 98457 023468
E-mail: *web@womensaid.org.uk*

Index